Sun
and
Purple

Silk and Purple

Lessons for Wives and Mothers from Women in the Old Testament

by CINDY HYLES SCHAAP

HYLES PUBLICATIONS
523 Sibley Street
Hammond, Indiana 46320

ISBN 0-9640504-0-4

Scripture references in this volume
are from the King James Bible.

Cover design by Keith Harrod,
Harrod Advertising, Chicago, IL

Printed and Bound in the United States of America

Dedication

Dedicated to my mother- and father-in-law, Ken and Marlene Schaap, who have added something irreplaceable to my life not only through rearing my husband, but also through their love and godly example.

Acknowledgements

I would like to acknowledge Linda Stubblefield and Angie Zachary for their help in typesetting and proofreading.

I cannot write a book without expressing appreciation to my mom and dad, who have a part in everything I am or have done. I thank them for the lessons they have taught me and for the many times they have allowed me to believe I discovered them on my own.

The same credit should go to my husband who has taught me a lot, not only by his life, but also by his knowledge of the Bible.

Contents

Preface

Cindy Schaap is my daughter. She is unique and special to Mrs. Hyles and me because she is our Hoosier girl. Our other three children were born in our home state of Texas; Cindy was born three months after our arrival in Hammond, Indiana. I watched her grow up. I remember her obedience to her mom and dad. I remember her soul-winning life as a teenager. I remember her prayer life. I remember going into her room without her knowing I was there and finding her on her knees praying beside her bed. I remember the times when she said she wasn't hungry, but I knew she was fasting and praying for some special need in the life of another. So for the first twenty years of her life, I saw her inside the walls of our home. She was all that a child and a teenager could be to her parents, to her church and to her Lord.

Now for the past fifteen years, I have mainly observed her only through the windows of her life; but after careful observance, I see her as being a wonderful wife, a godly and caring mother, a true woman of prayer, and a faithful and persistent soul winner. While she was growing up, we realized we were not training her for us but for someone else. As I peek through the windows of her life, I am confident that she is to that someone else what we trained her to be.

There are some areas, however, that I still observe from up close. First of all, I know what kind of daughter she is. She is an ideal daughter — one that gladdens the heart of her dad and mom and has made it all worthwhile.

I also see her up close as a church member. Once again, she is exactly what a pastor wants his lady church members to be — faithful, loyal, dedicated and spiritual.

Up close, I also see her as a pal and a buddy. Not only is she a member of my church and a member of my family, but she is a lot like the "girl-next-door" type. She is refreshing, friendly, intriguing, interesting and delightful.

Perhaps the closest relationship that Cindy and I have is that of friendship. We are, in the truest sense of the word, friends.

Cindy has not only made us proud of what she **is**, but of what she **does**. She has become an excellent college teacher, a superb ladies' speaker and a successful author, which you will confirm after reading this book.

—Dr. Jack Hyles

Introduction

"Thy word is a lamp unto my feet,
and a light unto my path."
(Psalm 119:105)

When I was eight years old, I began to read my Bible and pray on a pretty consistent daily basis. At that time, I began a personal friendship with Jesus Christ; and I also discovered my love for writing. This, I believe, was no coincidence. My first poem was written when I was eight years of age. It was entitled, "Always a Friend," speaking about my Friend, Jesus. During my teenage years, I continued my walk with the Lord. I sometimes wandered and I sometimes was inconsistent, but I kept going back to my Friend. He preserved me time and time again in spite of my being the rebellious teenager that I was.

I continued to walk with the Lord during my college days; of course, I was always encouraged to do so by the example and teachings of my parents. It was during my college days that I dated and married a preacher boy who was the person God had for me. I discovered that we shared a mutual love for walking with Christ.

During my newlywed days, I recognized my need to become a better wife and to have a better marriage. I knew the Bible was the place to turn for help, so I began to memorize the Bible more consistently. My Bible memory has meant so much to me through these years. It seems that each time I have started to write another article for *Christian Womanhood* or chapter for this book, a newly memorized verse has popped into my mind and has been appropriate for that particular lesson. It is the memorized verses that have spoken to me during some of the most difficult times I have endured as a preacher's daughter and as a preacher's wife. My Bible memory has changed my life.

As I approached my thirties, I became a bit confused in my Christian life about one issue in particular. I heard my husband preach a sermon in which he admonished his listeners to study the Bible, specifically the life of Jesus. Shortly thereafter, I became a student of the Bible which I had read and memorized for so many years. I studied the life of Jesus not using commentaries, but simply by writing in the flyleaf of my Bible everything about Jesus' life on earth which I could apply to my own. My confusion completely subsided, and my life has never been the same. I have studied the Bible on a pretty consistent basis ever since and my meditations of Him have been sweet. (See Psalm 104:34.) My Bible study has changed me as a wife and mother and, though I have much changing yet to be done, I am sure my husband would testify to that. I have heard him say so.

I have been asked several times why I am writing a book on the women of the Bible. My answer is this: "I am writing on the Bible because I love the Bible, and I am indebted to its Words." I am writing this book because I believe the Lord wants me to and because the idea impressed my husband whom I seek to please as much as I know how.

I am writing a book for wives and mothers because I want them to love the Bible more. I want them to see what is in the Bible for them. I am not a "deeper life" Christian. I not only feel a responsibility to know the Bible, but I am very committed to every Christian's responsibility to personal soul winning and to my responsibility to my husband and children. I want every wife and mother to discover with me just how much the Bible has to offer us in **all** of these areas — not in a "dry as dust" way, but in an exciting, up-to-date sort of way.

I am, at heart, not a writer but a housewife. I have only taken one I.Q. test and, though I am not sure how accurate it was, I found my I.Q. to be very average. I have taken no Greek or Hebrew classes, and I have not used much in the way of commentaries or outside sources as I have prepared this book. I say all of this simply to get across this point: The Bible is simple enough for everyone.

I have prayed for help before preparing each chapter and have analyzed the story of each lady to find helps for the wife and mother and for myself. I have used some supposition in order to relate each Bible woman with women of today. I am assuming that our human natures have not changed that much. If you disagree with my suppositions,I beg your mercy. I am, of course, not tampering with doctrine and would never attempt to do so.

I have used few outside sources, though I must give credit to the *Matthew Henry Commentary* and to the *Vine's Expository Dictionary of New Testament Words* which I have used occasionally. I have simply looked to find lessons from the words I saw in the King James Bible which might apply to the average Christian wife, mother and soul winner in 1994. I have been excited, surprised and enriched by the many lessons I have found.

There are some godless, deceived people in 1994 who seek to gradually change the Bible or to remove it from our minds. They say to the average person that the Bible is just not applicable to our daily lives anymore.

I wish we all would know the Bible for what it already is and not try to change it. If we did, we would all be richer in our marriages, in our families and in our ministries. I honestly love my King James Bible too much to ever change even a comma, and I have never had any difficulty understanding it. Though it is not mine to judge, I contend that those who seek to change the Bible could not possibly love it as I do. I love every word of the Bible, and I love the greatness of its unchangeable Author. I do not wish to play God by tampering with His Words, even with those which present ideas that are hard for me to understand.

My desire is not to emphasize Bible study at the expense of our service for Christ or our families. My desire is to emphasize how well Bible study complements our efforts as soul winners, wives and mothers. My desire is to encourage every reader to be a better wife, mother and soul winner by causing her to love the Bible as I do. If I fail to accomplish this mission, then I have failed the Word of God and its true purpose in the lives of Christian ladies.

Thank you for sharing this book with me!

Cindy Schaap
I Sam. 12:24

It's a Battle for the Bible

There are folks today who say they fight for choice and liberty,
But the words they speak don't fool this heart of mine.
It's the Bible they are after; it's the Christ Who died for me.
They are trying to remove them from our minds.

It's the Bible that is with me when my friends have walked
away.
It has carried me through sunshine and through storm.
It's the Bible that rebuked me when I sought to go astray.
It's the Word of God that gently, firmly warns.

I will stand up for the Bible for it's done so much for me.
I could never on its words or thoughts improve.
I will e'er obey its words that have been well-preserved for me.
They will hold me up and I shall not be moved.

CHORUS:
It's a battle for the Bible.
It's a battle for the Word of God.
I will stand up for the Bible.
I will stand up for the Word of God.

— Cindy Schaap

Eve —
A Lesson
on Dependence

*"My soul, wait thou only upon God;
for my expectation is from him."*
(Psalm 62:5)

Chapter 1
Eve
Genesis 2:18; 3:1 -16

$\mathcal{E}$VE MUST HAVE BEEN an extremely beautiful woman. She was God's original pattern from which all other women have come. In studying her life, every woman can understand a little bit more about herself and about womanhood in general. As God's first human creation, Adam must have been very handsome; and God made Eve to be Adam's perfectly suited match. Their relationship must have been very sweet! Even sweeter must have been the perfect fellowship between Eve and her God as they spoke audibly to each other in the cool of the garden.

Eve's home was a paradise. The Garden of Eden had everything necessary to make Eve happy, and it included nothing which would cause her any discomfort. Because I work outdoors in my own garden, I can appreciate the advantages of the Garden of Eden in a special way. Eve had the beautiful vegetables, fruits and flowers without the thorns, weeds and mosquitoes. In fact, it was a thunderstorm which led me into the house to write this chapter rather than to complete my half-finished yardwork, so I am a little envious of Eve right now! She had the flowers without the thorns and the sunshine without the thunderstorms. But Eve botched it all . . .

The devil came to Eve in the form of a serpent and asked

her if she was allowed to eat of every tree of the garden. Eve replied by saying she could eat of every tree except one. The devil got Eve to disobey God and to eat the forbidden fruit. How did he do this? He did it by telling Eve she would be like God. What was it that caused Eve to be attracted to such a promise? Was it her pride, or was it a sincere spiritual desire? I think it was a little bit of both. What I see in Eve leads me to make three observations about women in general and about myself in particular.

1. **Women (like me) are creatures full of pride**. Because of this, it is hard for us to ask for help from our authority.

2. **Women (like me) are spiritually aggressive creatures**. I believe that Eve was more naive than Adam — perhaps her hormones were changing. Eve's naivete caused her to be deceived and to really believe that she could become more spiritual if she ate of the fruit. Her aggressive nature caused her to jump at the chance of becoming more spiritual rather than to ask for help from her more logical husband or from her Creator.

3. **Women (like me) were created with natures which are *more* spiritually aggressive than men**. I can illustrate this through the spiritual natures of my own two children.

I began to teach my daughter, Jaclynn, about God when she was a very tiny girl. Since we had an extra chair at our dining room table at that time, I told Jaclynn that was Jesus' chair and that He would be there sitting with our family at every dinner hour. Jaclynn's emotional nature causes her to readily accept things which she cannot see. Therefore, she quickly believed that Jesus was in that chair, that He was everywhere. He became her special Friend. (One time, Jaclynn even told a guest who was occupying Jesus' chair that she was sitting on Jesus!)

Kenny was just as young when I told him the very same things about Jesus. "Kenny," I said, "Jesus is here; Jesus is everywhere." Kenny's logical mind caused him to respond in this manner. "He is not here. I can't see Him."

I have worked and prayed to see that Kenny would accept the reality of God, and I believe that he has as much as a 9-year-old boy can; but I realize that there are major differences between the way a male and a female perceive things spiritually.

Often I hear of a woman who is very involved in church who has a husband who is not involved in church at all. Rarely do I hear of a man who is involved in church whose wife is not. It happens occasionally, but rarely.

In fact, Adam himself is the best illustration of the lack of spiritual aggression on the part of men. God commanded Adam to dress and keep the garden in Genesis 2:15. The word *keep* means to *protect*. God told Adam that his job was to not only bear fruit in the garden, but also to protect it. From what was Adam to protect the Garden of Eden? There were no dangerous animals, no mass murderers, no boogeymen. Adam was to protect the Garden of Eden from the devil. However, not only did Adam allow the devil to enter the Garden of Eden, but Adam also remained awfully quiet when the conversation between Eve and the devil took place. What was Adam's role in Eve's temptation? He had no role. After Eve had succumbed, Adam's role became that of a follower as he was led by Eve into sin.

With Eve as the leader and Adam as the follower, trouble took place. That is why I believe that God defined Adam and Eve's roles in the Garden of Eden. He made Adam the leader and Eve the follower. Though God defined Adam and Eve's **roles**, I do not believe that He changed their **natures**. Eve continued to be the more spiritually aggressive with a desire to make quick, emotional and impulsive decisions. Adam continued to be less spiritually aggressive and to be hesitant to take the lead.

Why did God give men and women roles which are so contrary to their natures? I believe it was because God wanted men and women to depend upon Him. When Adam's role was that of follower, he was able to shake responsibility. Perhaps he had no tremendous sense of his need for God because he had no one really depending upon him. Since the fall of man, things have been quite different for the male race — especially for the male who seeks to follow Christ in his family role. Man is now the leader, and he must depend on God to help him know how to do that which is not always natural for him. It **is not** natural for a man to be a leader because he is born a follower. The most important person in the male's first years of life is his mother, a female who tells him when to brush his teeth, when to go to bed, when to eat, etc. When a male becomes a husband, his role changes. He must assume a role for which he is often unprepared. If he is to assume and perform that role the way in which God would have him to, he must depend totally upon God.

When a female becomes a wife, she continues the role of dependence which should have begun for her in the father/daughter relationship. Often, though, a female has no father who will teach her this proper spiritual role which God designed for her. If he does teach her, as my father did, she will still spend her entire life battling the aggressive nature which God has given to her. I know! I have been happily married for 15 years. The hardest thing I do as a wife is to keep my mouth shut when decisions need to be made. My husband will tell you that it is a difficult thing for me to do. Yet he will also tell you, I believe, that I am learning more and more how to follow as he is learning more and more how to lead. How have we learned this? We have learned more and more about our respective roles through our daily walk with God as we become more and more dependent upon Him. If I miss just a few days of my dependent walk with God, I find that I become aggressive and bold in areas where I should be submissive and sweet.

In the next few chapters and throughout this book, I will make much reference to the importance of a wife's submission in the home. I will discuss some of the results that occur when a wife is not submissive. Let me say, however, that I have no desire to be condemning or judgmental as I cover these subjects. I know that submission is very difficult. It is hard for me; it was hard for Eve. Please remember this as you continue reading.

I believe God knew all of this would be hard for us. I also believe He set up the roles as He did so that His creation would learn to depend upon Him. Without our dependence on God, we are apt to make even poorer decisions than Eve did in the Garden of Eden.

So, every morning, you'll find me somewhere on my knees asking God to help me submit to my husband. Somewhere not far away, you'll find my husband alone on his knees asking for strength and wisdom to lead his family. With our dependence upon God, we have found our God-given roles to be most satisfying. Without our dependence upon God, our marriage, our children, our own lives would — like Eve's — certainly be lost forever.

Noah's Wife —
A Lesson
on Persecution

*"Yea, and all that will live godly
in Christ Jesus shall suffer persecution."*
(II Timothy 3:12)

Chapter 2
Noah's Wife
Genesis 6:1 -8:22

*N*OAH'S WIFE IS ONE whom I had not originally planned to include in my book on Bible women but, in a short span of time, I had three friends mention to me that they hoped I would include her. Not much is directly mentioned about Noah's wife. In fact, we do not even know her name. I hesitate to write about her because I am hesitant to speculate about things the Bible does not actually say. However, what she went through makes Noah's wife a truly interesting Bible character.

Genesis 6:8 and 9 tell us that Noah found grace in the eyes of the Lord and that Noah was a just and perfect man who walked with God. Knowing what I have come to understand about the influence a wife has over her husband, I have no doubt that Noah's wife was a just woman also. I believe that she was just and that she walked with God especially because she stood with Noah through great persecution.

I have been through some bit of persecution with my preacher father and with our family, and I well know what it takes to endure such persecution. It takes a close walk with God. If it is necessary for me to walk with God to stay faithful in my trivial times of persecution, it surely was a necessary thing for Noah's wife and her character. God did, after all, expect Noah's wife to stand beside her husband as he did some strange and unusual things.

God told Noah to build a large boat called an ark in order to spare Noah and his family from the flood of water which God would send. God intended to destroy the entire world and all its people through this flood. As far as we know, it had never before rained even a drop on the earth. Imagine how strange it must have seemed to Noah's wife as she looked out the window to the back yard and saw her husband and sons building a huge boat, complete with rooms for their family as well as for two of every kind of animal. I wonder if she ever walked away from the window in confusion wondering if she was really doing what God would have her to do in the situation by keeping her mouth shut and following her husband.

Imagine what the neighbors thought about the whole thing! Since Noah was a just man, I feel sure he approached his friends and neighbors about the coming flood, hoping they would join him in the ark and be saved. This was not God's plan, however. The devil had his deadly grip on the rest of the world, and God allowed him to do his damage. God described the other citizens of Noah's world as being wicked and having thoughts which were evil continually. There could have been no room for spiritual discernment in their wicked minds. It would have been impossible for them to comprehend God's warning to Noah. They did not fear God and, therefore, probably felt no guilt as they taunted and jeered Noah and his family as they built their ark.

But Noah's wife stayed true. She stayed true enough to follow Noah right into that ark as well as to influence her sons and daughters-in-law to follow also. She stayed true enough to help care for two of every kind of animal on earth, a male and a female. (This may not have been the most spiritual aspect of her submission, but it is truly the most amazing to me. After all, **one** pet in the house is trouble enough!)

It is difficult to stay true to those we love when we find ourselves sharing with them in persecution. I know this by experience, and I know that it is a walk with God which helps us to stay true. My own walk with God has kept me faithful to those I love time after time when I found it to be difficult. I remember the morning of August 25, 1985. Criticism had been hurled toward my family, and I hurt deeply. I turned to the place I have been turning with my troubles since I was eight years old. I turned to the Word of God. Because it was the 25th of the month, part of my Bible reading that day included the 25th Proverb. God led me there to Proverbs 25:19 which says, *"Confidence in an unfaithful man in time of trouble is like a broken tooth, and a foot out of joint."* I am looking at that verse as I write this chapter. It is circled and has the previously mentioned date written above it. It was that day and in that place of my beloved Bible when I decided I would, above all, be faithful to my parents, to my pastor and to my husband even when it brought pain. I would not run; my love would not change in time of trouble.

Troubles have come again and again since that summer day; and though I am no great lady like Noah's wife, I have a walk with the same God with Whom she walked, and I have stayed faithful to those I love. This is to my amazement and to God's glory. During these times of trouble and persecution, I have learned several things that a walk with God can do. Each time my heart is deeply wounded, it seems that God takes me through the same steps. Everyone who is used of God or who has a loved one who is used of God will suffer persecution, especially as our world grows worse and worse. It is my desire that all Christians would be true to God and to their friends even when times are hard. I want to share what God can do for those who walk with Him during those difficult times by telling you what my walk with God does for me.

1. My walk with God gives me *strength* to carry on. The first thing I learned as an adult going through criticism and persecution is that I am a coward. I do not like to be hated; I do not even like to think that others do not like me. I learned through persecution how really weak I am.

My husband will tell you that attacks from the devil upon

our family bring me to tears — lots of tears. The only thing that helps this coward and this crybaby to go on is that I know where to run when I am afraid. I run to the Lord.

My first response to the hurt is, "Lord, I can't go on." When I say I can't go on, I mean exactly that. I mean that I have no strength to do the simple, daily tasks of life. When I am hurt from persecution, I cannot cook dinner, I cannot take a bath, etc. So I pray and pray and pray. Then God takes me to step one. He gives me strength to go on. I have been there time and time again. I still have no faith, no hope and no peace; but I **do** have strength to go on. I am always surprised to find after my prayer time with God that I indeed **can** go on. God gives me that strength.

2. My walk with God gives me *peace*. As I go on in God's strength through my daily chores, a peace settles upon me. Persecution has caused the word *peace* to have a more personal meaning in my life. Peace is when the worrying and the crying cease and pleasant thoughts of God calm my spirit. I still cannot find hope or faith in the situation at hand, but it doesn't really matter. I have sought the Lord, and He has rushed to my side once more to be my Comforter. Once more I can sing in the quietness of my soul a song which has come to mean so much to me.

Wonderful Peace

Far away in the depths of my spirit tonight,
Rolls a melody sweeter than psalm;
In celestial-like strains it unceasingly falls
O'er my soul like an infinite calm.

Peace! Peace! Wonderful peace,
Coming down from the Father above;
Sweep over my spirit forever, I pray,
In fathomless billows of love.

— W. D. Cornell

3. My walk with God gives me *faith*. I do not see any

hope for the situation yet, but I suddenly believe that God can work good even if I can't see it at the time. I no longer must **constantly** seek the Lord for comfort (though I don't need God any less). I can now turn my spirit toward serving others for my spirit of faith has been renewed. With that renewed faith comes renewed joy which I can in turn share with others once again.

4. My walk with God gives me *hope*. How sweet the moment when hope rises in my soul, that moment when I can see the dawning of exactly what good might take place through this persecution. Often this hope comes quite a while before any answered prayer, but the greatness of God is eventually proven once again in my personal life as answers to prayer arrive.

5. My walk with God gives me *love*. He gives me love to care for others who hurt more than I do, the love of God I need to be a faithful woman in time of trouble. Best of all, and slowest in coming I might add, is the love which God sends for my persecutors, those who have brought hurt to my life and to the lives of my loved ones. What a wonderful feeling it is! I think it to be the greatest feeling in all the earth. To look in your soul and find love where there should be hatred and bitterness is perhaps the greatest result of a walk with God. It brings the knowledge that God still works miracles and that He is working a miracle inside of me.

I did not give you these five points so that you would pity me. There is an old saying: "If all of our troubles were hung on a line, you would take yours and I would take mine." God has been so good to all of us and, in His goodness, He has allowed us to suffer trouble. If God has used us, the devil has persecuted our souls. I share these steps with you so that you might learn patience during that persecution, the patience you will need to stay faithful to those you love. How thankful I am for God's working in my life, allowing me to stay faithful to those who have been so faithful to me.

It must have felt awfully warm and cozy inside the ark when the rain started falling. I can imagine the reverence and the fear of God that Noah's wife must have felt when she stepped off the ark and heard the eerie quiet, realizing that God had saved her family and hers alone. Her and her family's response was to do what they had done so many times before; they fell to their knees and communed with their God. How thankful Noah's wife must have been that she had remained faithful to her husband! How thankful she must have been that her family had not perished in the world! How thankful she must have been for her walk with God which had led her thus far to endure persecution and suffering! How thankful I am also for my walk with God and all it has so wonderfully brought me through!

Lot's Wife —
A Lesson on Worldliness

❧

*"Love not the world, neither the things
that are in the world.
If any man love the world,
the love of the Father is not in him."*
(I John 2:15)

"Remember Lot's wife."
(Luke 17:32)

Chapter 3
Lot's Wife
Genesis 19:1-26

*T*HE STORY OF LOT'S wife is one of the most unusual in the Bible. It begins with a fight between Abraham's herdsmen and Lot's herdsmen. Because the two groups of men could not get along, Abraham and his nephew, Lot, decided to go their separate ways. The beginning of Lot's backsliding into worldliness seems to have started when Lot chose the well-watered plains of Jordan for himself instead of leaving the best for the elder, his Uncle Abraham.

I have no doubt that it was Lot's wife who influenced Lot to choose the best for himself without considering God's will, but considering only what material, earthly benefits Sodom had to offer. I believe this for two reasons. First, I believe it because after studying the subject of marriage and teaching it for ten years, I am aware of the amazing influence that every wife has on her husband. Secondly, I believe it because it was Lot's **wife** who most hated to leave Sodom.

Perhaps Lot's wife was tired of dwelling in tents and thought that Sodom would be a good place to build a house. Perhaps she could look out the door of her tent in the evenings and see the exciting night life of Sodom. Regardless of the reason Lot chose Sodom, I am quite certain that his wife had something to do with that choice.

It is also certain that the influence of Lot's wife continued to be a bad one while this couple actually lived in Sodom. We do not know a lot about their years in Sodom, but we do know that Lot and his wife did not share Christ in soul winning with even four people while they were there. The Bible says that Lot was a "just" man which indicates that he was a saved man. If Lot's wife and his four daughters were saved, then they would have had to lead only four other people to the Lord in order for the city of Sodom to have been spared. When Abraham interceded in behalf of Sodom, God promised that he would spare the city if ten righteous people could be found therein. (Genesis 18:20-33) Because ten righteous people could **not** be found, Sodom was destroyed with fire and brimstone.

Perhaps Lot's wife was simply too busy redecorating her home or going to parties to do much witnessing. She must have been too busy to witness even to her own sons-in-law or, if they were saved, she was too busy to influence them very much spiritually. Her two sons-in-law refused to listen to Lot when he told them that Sodom was going to be burned. Instead, they chose to stay in the city where they would soon be killed.

The Bible says that the sins in Sodom vexed (grieved) Lot's soul, and yet Lot was **unable** to stand up for what was right and to leave the city. Again, I can't help but imagine that his wife had a lot of influence in this decision.

The most startling part of this story took place when two angels came to Sodom. The Bible says in Genesis 19:4 that **all** of the men in the city showed up to try to force themselves upon these two angels in an attempt to commit a homosexual act. Lot tried to protect the angels in his own house, but the men of the city tried to break down the door in an effort to have their evil way with the angels. Lot's corruption was most vividly displayed when he offered his own two virgin daughters for the men of the city to do with them what was good in their eyes. The angels saved the two innocent, victimized daughters by smiting the men of the city with blindness. However, the blindness did not stop these men from burning in their lust toward the angels and continuing to at least try to find the door.

This story is one of the most revolting in the Bible. It is hard to imagine the fear that would be going through my mind if such an experience were to take place at my own house. It is difficult to understand how a city and **all** of its men could be so corrupt. Most unbelievable of all is that Lot and his wife were so steeped in the wickedness of Sodom that they were willing to offer their own virgin daughters as sex partners with such lustful and beastly men. You would think that it would be with great delight that this family would take off out of there the next day . . . but such was not the case.

Perhaps Lot's wife was thinking about the home which her family had just finished having built. Maybe she was thinking about a room in that home which had just been recently remodeled or about how much she would miss her position at the clubs. Possibly she had a new dress in her closet which she had never been able to wear. It might have seemed a shame to her for it to go to waste. Whatever her thinking, Lot's wife disobeyed and did what she had been warned not to do. She turned around and took one last, longing look at her burning hometown. When she did this, she was turned into a pillar of salt and her life was gone completely.

Incredible! Why did she stay in Sodom so long in the first place? Why was she not **thrilled** to be leaving such a wicked city after what had happened the night before? Why was she not thinking about her husband and her daughters who would need her so much after what they were now going through? Great is my disgust and dismay with Lot's wife until I realize one thing . . . I AM JUST LIKE LOT'S WIFE!

No, I have never been through the experiences this woman went through, but I'm afraid we do have something in common. I also am often too steeped in my love for the world in which I now live. I am not sure why. My world is also wicked. Millions of babies are murdered every year in the land in which I live. Homosexuality is a major problem in my world, and all kinds of immorality are becoming more and more prevalent, even among teenagers and children. We have a gang problem, a drug problem and a murder problem. Children carry guns to school and are given birth control devices, but they are not allowed to read their Bibles or to pray. God is viewed as a myth in my land, and Satan is worshiped by more people than ever before.

I don't want to love a world such as this . . . but I do. So, I want to learn from Lot's wife. I do not **wish** to love this world nor to fit in with it as she did. I wish to make an impact on my world — the impact that Lot's wife **should** have made. I do not wish to see my family nor my own life destroyed. I wish to live a life that glorifies Christ. The following are some things that we can learn from Lot's wife which will help us to avoid the outcome which was hers:

1. **Never choose a place to live outside of God's will**. Four-and-a-half years after my husband and I married, I became "itchy" to get a new house. I went to my husband and told him my desire. In so many words, he told me that we would never move out of the house we were in unless God directly led us to do so. He also told me that we would never seek material things in our ministry.

I was not mature enough spiritually to make these decisions at the time. But I **was** mature enough to follow my husband. God **did** lead us to a new home shortly thereafter, but it **was** God's direct leading. Now we are happy in a home where we plan to stay until God kicks us out. We feel the same way about the place where we serve the Lord. God led us to the place where we serve, and we will not even think about leaving unless He directly leads my husband elsewhere. Lot's wife would have been better off if she had considered God's will and followed her husband rather than influencing him to choose the well-watered plains.

2. **Make it a priority in your life to influence others for Christ, to take a stand**. Soul winning is a good way to take a stand for Christ. When you go door-to-door soul winning, you get a chance to see the world and what it really has to offer. You see a lot of heartache. You also receive a lot of persecution. A

soul winner is not tempted to love the world as much because the world does not love soul winners. If we take a stand for Christ, we will be less tempted to love the world. If we **are** steeped in worldliness, our children and those who follow us will see the hypocrisy of our Christian lives and will not want to adopt our standards.

Perhaps if Lot's wife had taken a stand for Christ, she would have had Christian sons-in-law; and she could have spared an entire community through her personal soul winning.

3. **Stay away from television and other worldly influences which will harden your heart to sin**. In the past few years, I have basically lived by a "no television" philosophy. Because of this, if I turn on the television at all in order to watch a football game or the news, I am appalled by what I see — especially in advertisements. I am ashamed to say that when I watched more television in the past, I became hardened to much of the sin that I saw.

I often speak with Christians whose language, dress standards and philosophies betray the fact that they have been hardened to the awfulness of sin. When I consider the types of things that they might be seeing on television, in secular books and magazines, on the radio, etc., I realize that it is no wonder so many Christians act and look so much like the world. Their familiarity with the world has hardened them to the disgusting qualities of sin.

When I see the type of sin to which Lot and his wife grew accustomed, I do not even want to begin this process.

4. **Always place people before things**. The wife of Dr. Wendell Evans (President of Hyles-Anderson College) is Mrs. Marlene Evans. She explains this same idea in a way that I love: **"Like things** and **love people**. Don't love things and like people."** It is natural for us as human beings to like things to a certain extent. However, when we allow ourselves to love things and to put them before people, we subject ourselves to worldliness. *"For the love of money is the root of all evil."* (I

Timothy 6:10a)

It is my belief that Lot's wife loved things like the well-watered plains of Sodom and only liked things like her daughters, their husbands and her unsaved neighbors. Because of this, she neglected to influence them for Christ and for right. Her own life was ruined when she became a pillar of salt. Her married daughters and their husbands were destroyed in Sodom's fire, and her two virgin daughters and Lot were destroyed by drunkenness and incest. It is no wonder! They had no mother to be a positive spiritual influence on their home.

I fight in my own life the desire to love money and materialistic things. I see the scratches on the legs of my coffee table and wonder when I'll be able to replace the table. I feel frustration in knowing that those scratches came from the carelessness of a rough and rugged little boy who lives at our house. It is then that I remind myself to **love people** and to **like things**. The little boy is more important than the coffee table. I must remember that a few scratches on the furniture are a small price to pay for that which is really important.

Though I do not wish to abuse my home, I do wish to allow myself and my loved ones to use it. Most of all, I do not want to put my house above the needs of my family. I want instead to be there for them, influencing them spiritually — especially in their time of sorrow and need.

5. **Remember Lot's wife**. The best advice I can give you about Lot's wife is given in the Bible in Luke 17:32 which says, *"Remember Lot's wife."* When we are tempted toward materialism, we must remember that it leads to worldliness. We must remember Lot's wife and remember that worldliness leads to a hardening toward the awfulness of sin. We then need to remind ourselves that the hardening of our hearts toward sin leads to the destruction of our own lives and of the lives of our family members.

Perhaps Lot's wife was **not** looking back on Sodom because she wanted to see a new house one more time. Maybe she did

not miss her clubs or a new dress. Perhaps she did **not** long for
a last look at a newly remodeled room. Perhaps she was looking
back with regret. Conceivably she was longing for one last look
at her two daughters who would burn to death in Sodom with
her unbelieving sons-in-law. Perhaps there were grandchildren
involved who felt the torture of fire and brimstone. Whatever the
reason, she disobeyed God when she looked at Sodom, and she
was turned into a pillar of salt. We are forever admonished to
"remember Lot's wife." Remember the price she paid for her
worldliness. Remember the twisted plot of her life. Remember
the broken lives of her family. Remember her death. Remember
her regret. *"Remember Lot's wife."*

Sarah —
A Lesson on Faith

*"For whosoever will save his life shall lose it;
but whosoever shall lose his life for my sake
and the gospel's, the same shall save it."*
(Mark 8:35)

*"Through faith also Sara herself received strength
to conceive seed, and was delivered of a child
when she was past age, because she judged
him faithful who had promised."*
(Hebrews 11:11)

Chapter 4
Sarah
Genesis 12, 16, 21

SARAH IS PROBABLY THOUGHT of as one of the greatest Christian ladies in the Bible. She was married to Abraham, one of the greatest leaders in the Bible. She became the mother of a great nation, Israel. Yet when I read about Sarah's life in the Word of God, I find that she was a very typical lady. In fact, most of what can be found in the Bible about Sarah is sort of negative.

Twice in the Bible, we find Sarah lying by telling two different kings that she was Abraham's sister. Actually, Sarah wasn't really lying; she was merely telling only part of the truth. You see, Abraham **was** Sarah's half-brother; but she failed to mention that he was also her husband. Sarah's exaggeration was sin, and it almost got her into serious trouble. Still, I find Sarah's exaggeration to be encouraging to someone like myself who tends to stretch the story a little bit sometimes. I try very hard to be honest; in fact, preachers' kids are prone to be extremely forthright. Yet I, like Sarah, am a typical woman and am still working on ridding myself of the sin of exaggeration.

Later in the Bible, we find Sarah laughing at the Word of God. God sent three angels to Abraham telling him that he and Sarah would have a son. Sarah overheard them talking and laughed out loud. When the angels asked why Sarah had laughed, Sarah became afraid and denied that she had. There she was, lying again. Not only did Sarah lie this time, but she revealed two emotions which I have often felt in my own life: fear and lack of faith.

Fear has been an emotion with which I have had to deal through the years. I was horribly afraid of thunderstorms when I was a little girl. I was so afraid that I even panicked at the sight of a semi-dark sky. I had a strong fear of staying home alone while my husband traveled until one day God delivered me from it. I can't explain why or how, but after years of praying for deliverance from this fear, one day I was no longer afraid. Yet I must admit that when a raccoon crawled up on our roof recently, I woke my daughter, Jaclynn, to see if she would help me check and **just be sure** that it really was just a raccoon. I couldn't get up the nerve to check by myself. I guess faith is the antidote for fear and, as you can tell from this illustration, I lack it myself sometimes. I guess I am a typical Christian in some ways, just like Sarah was.

Sarah became impatient with God's plans for her life — so impatient that she gave her maid, Hagar, to bear a child for Abraham. I understand impatience. I try to keep the speed limit; I really think I ought to keep it. But sometimes when I am in a hurry . . . I am always in a hurry and have a hard time understanding people who are not. I am learning not to try to hurry God and His plans for my life, but I have not arrived in this area; I am still learning.

Sarah was jealous. How typical of a member of the female gender! She gave her maid, Hagar, to her husband and Hagar bore Abraham a son, Ishmael; then Sarah got jealous and kicked out Hagar and Ishmael from the house. I have struggled with jealousy in my own life. I pray daily that God will give me the victory over comparing myself with other women and other Christians. I am learning to accept myself the way God has made me, but sometimes the dreaded green-eyed monster creeps back into my life. After admitting all of these weaknesses, I suppose you would believe me to be a weak Christian at best.

Knowing that Sarah shares all of these weaknesses with me makes her a very typical Christian lady . . . yet Sarah became the mother of God's favored nation. The Bible tells us that she was still very beautiful when she was past ninety years of age. Most surprising of all, God lists Sarah as a hero of the faith in Hebrews 11:11 and 12. *"Through faith also Sara herself received strength to conceive seed, and was delivered of a child when she was past age, because she judged him faithful who had promised. Therefore sprang there even of one, and him as good as dead, so many as the stars of the sky in multitude, and as the sand which is by the sea shore innumerable."* My question is this: "Why Sarah?" Did she really have **great** faith? I think not! Sarah had only a little bit of faith, yet she acted upon the little bit of faith she had rather than on her unbelief.

How did she act upon her faith? Through submission! The one good characteristic I can find about Sarah is that she seemed to follow her husband through thick and thin, always doing what Abraham told her to do. I believe this demonstrates what great faith really is; great faith is simply a little bit of faith invested through the action of obedience. That is why I believe the key to great faith is a little bit of faith plus obedience. Put simply:

LITTLE FAITH + OBEDIENCE = GREAT FAITH

The key to a married woman having great faith is found in her obedience to her own husband.

Not only do I learn from Sarah's life much about obedience and great faith, but I also learn much about what to do when my vision, or that in which I have put my faith, dies.

God told Abraham that he would be the father of a great nation. I can just imagine Sarah's excitement when Abraham came to her with the great news. Perhaps she was just a young woman at the time, and every young woman has great expectations about becoming a mother and about the potential of the children she will bear. It seems that all young husbands and wives start families filled with anticipation about what God is going to do, if not through their own lives and marriages, then surely through the lives of their offspring. But dreams of youth do not always become the realities of tomorrow, as Sarah and Abraham discovered.

When Sarah got into her thirties, she may have begun to doubt a little bit. Perhaps she clung to a hope because, after all, thirty is not really beyond childbearing years and Abraham was such a good husband. She knew he would not have imagined the dream he had been carrying for all of these years.

When Sarah got into her forties, I imagine many tears were shed. Perhaps she began to doubt God and the veracity of His Word. Maybe she became a little bit critical of Abraham in her heart. After all, she had followed him everywhere, leaving her homeland and everything she held dear, and why? She did it because Abraham was clinging to a dream which seemed elusive. Maybe she wished she could run back home to the old life, yet she stayed; she continued to obey; she continued to follow. Sarah continued to hope and to act upon her little bit of faith.

Perhaps the fifties, sixties, seventies and eighties passed by with Sarah giving up hope altogether. She resigned herself to the fact that Abraham's dream probably would not come to pass. Her little bit of faith told her that it still could be, but her growing, maturing love for Abraham and for her God told her it didn't really matter. She would stay and she would follow, and what would be would be.

To be honest with you, I have just taken you through a lifetime which is comparable to the lives of many servants of God. The names are different as are the places. The dreams are different, but the scenario is similar. God gave each of these Christians a dream, and each one held onto the dream until it finally died. Some Hall-of-Fame type Christians have experienced the death of a dream similar to that of Abraham and Sarah. Men like Joseph, Moses, the disciples and even Jesus Christ Himself all saw the dream for which they had lived die before it came to life again.

These men, other than Jesus, of course, did not know that their dreams would be resurrected. They simply acted upon what faith they had left by obeying until their dreams were fulfilled.

God usually kills a vision before He fulfills it. He does this so that He can create in those He uses a character which is worthy of the fulfillment. He also does it so that He can get the glory. If God had fulfilled all of Sarah's dreams when she was young, her tendency to exaggerate might have caused her to take the credit herself. If God had fulfilled every dream that I had as a young adult, I would have taken too much of the glory upon myself — of that I am sure. I also would have never had the opportunity to learn to love God with the depth which says, "When You disappoint me and kill my dreams, I will still love You with a maturing love. Lord, whatever You would have to be in my life, let it be."

The most crucial time in a marriage or in any other relationship is that time when the dreams of youth have died. Most newlyweds experience a very shallow type of love. Their lives are held together by a dream — perhaps of a house, a car, children, a career or best of all, a ministry. If the dream that holds them together dies, they must learn to love because of character and commitment. They must learn to die to self. They must stay together while this new type of love is developing in their lives. They must continue to obey God's Word which forbids divorce and adultery. They must act upon their little bit of faith. When children of God act upon their little bit of faith, God will reward them by doing one of three things in their lives.

1. **God will replace their dreams with something better**. God has killed some of the dreams my husband and I had in our youth. In some cases, He has already replaced them with something better.

Perhaps a couple dreams of starting a great church and seeing it grow and prosper. God may replace that dream with the reality of a godly son who will pastor a great church. Perhaps a couple dreams of rearing godly children. God may replace that dream with a ministry to the children of others. Whatever God does, it will be surprising — and it will be far beyond what mere humans could imagine. There will be a time, however, between the death of the old dream and the resurrection of the new when the couple must love and obey because of their little bit of faith.

2. **God will replace their dreams with a special relationship with Him**. I do not wish this point to be an excuse for those who would be lazy and slothful in God's work while contenting themselves with studying God's Word to the exclusion of **doing** something for God. Yet there are many times when our capacities — maybe due to poor health — do not measure up to our dreams. God perhaps gives us a dream and then allows it to die so that we might draw closer to Him. I have seen in my life the death of some dreams which have **not** been replaced with something better. During these times of death to self, I have become more aware of God's presence in my life and have truly received the greatest blessing of all. I believe we will find some fulfilled dreams waiting when we get to Heaven. We will discover ways that God used us, possibly in spite of health problems, which He could not reveal to us on earth.

3. **God will fulfill the dream**. Some of my dreams have seen fulfillment and, oh, how sweet has been that fulfillment! Sometimes, it seemed to me that God was slow in fulfilling my dreams and in answering my prayers. Yet, when He did answer, His timing seemed so perfect.

Sarah was one of those fortunate ones who saw her dream fulfilled while she was still on earth. God rewarded Sarah for her little bit of faith by allowing her to see her husband's dream exactly fulfilled in a miraculous way when little Isaac was born to a mother in her nineties. Abraham **did** become the father of a great nation, and Sarah's old age was crowned with a beautiful face that only the serenity of faith and obedience could decorate.

When it was all said and done, maybe Sarah's weakness of exaggeration caused her to proclaim, "I knew all along it would turn out this way." Yet, I think not! I think Sarah looked to the

Heavens with a mature and deep love for her God and said, "To God be all the glory!" Then perhaps she looked to her aged husband, Abraham, and said to herself in a satisfied way, "I really did love him, didn't I?" Whatever her reaction, I am sure she was glad that she had continued to follow and to love regardless of the consequences. I am sure that she did not regret acting upon the little bit of faith she never lost. I pray that all of God's servants, including myself, would do the same.

Hagar —
A Lesson on Loneliness

❧

"And be content with such things as ye have:
for he hath said, I will never leave thee,
nor forsake thee."
(Hebrews 13:5b)

Chapter 5
Hagar
Genesis 16, 21:9-21

Dedicated to forsaken wives,
whose cry God hears

HAGAR WAS SARAH'S MAID who was given to Abraham to be his wife. Because Sarah was childless, she encouraged this marriage; this was her way of scheming to make Abraham the father of a great nation. The Bible says that when Hagar found that she was with child, Sarah was despised in her eyes. Hagar probably realized that she had been used to get Sarah and Abraham what they wanted and that this marriage had not been a union of love at all. Most men and women can understand at least a little bit of Hagar's feelings, having at some time been forsaken by a friend or a loved one.

Of course, Hagar's attitude toward Sarah bothered her mistress. Perhaps Hagar's presence and her spiteful look made Sarah realize the seriousness of her wrongdoing. Perhaps it just hurt Sarah's pride. In any case, Sarah made known to Abraham that something was wrong, and Abraham gave Sarah permission to do as she pleased with Hagar. Sarah was very hard in her dealings with Hagar, and Hagar ran away from Sarah and Abraham. Here we have the story of the first marital separation in the Bible. It is the story of an abused and forsaken little handmaid.

Hagar did what every abused or forsaken wife should do. She called upon the Lord in her loneliness. Genesis 16:13 tells us that Hagar looked after the Lord in the wilderness. God cared about this lonely little expectant mother, and He sent an angel to minister to her. The angel encouraged Hagar to return to Abraham and Sarah. The angel told Hagar that she would bring forth a child and that she should name the child *Ishmael* meaning, *the Lord hath heard thy affliction*. Ishmael, the angel said, would be a wild man and would be the father of a great nation. Hagar, recognizing the love of God in her time of need, named the angel which spoke to her and the place where he spoke, *"thou God seest me."* Hagar then returned to her husband.

Some time later, however, another son was born to Hagar's husband. This time, it was Sarah who bore Abraham a son. This was the promised son from God, Isaac. About the time that Isaac was weaned, Sarah requested of Abraham that Hagar and her young son be kicked out of the household. Sarah did not want this "lower-class citizen" to be in competition with her son for any type of inheritance. Abraham grieved deeply for his son, Ishmael, but God told Abraham to hearken to the voice of Sarah.

The next morning, Abraham sent Hagar and Ishmael away with a bottle of water and some bread. The Bible says that Hagar and the child wandered in the wilderness of Beer-sheba. They didn't know where to go or what to do, so they just existed in a state of wandering nowhere. I'm sure that many forsaken wives understand what it means to just wander.

It didn't take long for Hagar to run out of bread and water for herself and her son. When she did, she threw her child under a shrub in despair. Not only was Hagar forsaken by her husband and her employer, but she was desperate enough financially to forsake her own child. It wasn't that she didn't love her child. It was just that she saw no way to care for him, and she could not stand to see him suffer. Hagar sat down just a bowshot away from her child and began to weep.

Hagar did something else though, and her actions saved both herself and her son. She began to cry unto the Lord. Then the Bible says that God heard the cry of the child, Ishmael. I love the fact that though it was the grown woman who shouted out unto the Lord, God was listening to the cry of the child. Jesus has a special place in His heart for children and teenagers. I have always believed that a person's attitude toward children reflects in a great way that person's character. God, Who is perfect in His character, heard the cry of the first child of divorce.

God heard the forsaken child, and then He spoke to the forsaken wife. He asked her the precious, and yet simple, question that every parent asks when he sees his beloved child weeping, "What's the matter?" God, of course, knew what was the matter; He just wanted to give Hagar the chance to talk about it.

What was God's first command to the first divorced and forsaken mother? It was *"fear not."* God wanted this forsaken wife and mother to know that she did not need to be afraid. God assured Hagar that He had heard the cry of her son. How precious! God knows that the major concern of every God-fearing single mother is not for herself, but for her children. God comforted Hagar not for herself, but where He knew she needed it most. God promised Hagar that Ishmael would be the father of a great nation, and He encouraged Hagar to pick up the child and hold him. Then God provided a well of water for Hagar and 'met the needs of her child.

The Bible says that *"God was with the lad; and he grew, and dwelt in the wilderness, and became an archer."* (Genesis 21:20)

There are so many sweet lessons contained in this story which apply to the forsaken wife and to her children.

1. **The separated woman should seek the Lord in her loneliness**.

2. **The separated woman should return to her husband if he will still have her**.

3. **The separated woman should realize God sometimes allows people to be forsaken**. It was startling for me the first time I realized it was God who encouraged Abraham to cast out Hagar. Abraham went against God when he took another wife and tried to fulfill God's promises in his own way. This unholy union brought about two great nations which could not exist together under one roof. To this day, the ancestors of these two boys cannot get along. God, therefore, allowed Hagar to be forsaken.

The New Testament clearly teaches that God is against divorce. Allowance is made for divorce in cases of adultery because of the hardness of the heart. This means that God will permit divorces if those betrayed by adultery are unwilling to forgive. Yet, I believe God never intends divorce, even in the cases of adultery.

Hagar should not have married Abraham in the first place, but perhaps she felt she had to do so. Nevertheless, we must remember that God **allowed** Hagar to be forsaken. Ignorance regarding polygamy was winked at in the Old Testament times and would be treated differently today. Yet it was God Who **told** Abraham to cast out Hagar. What can we learn from this when we cannot completely understand the mind of God? We can learn exactly that! We **cannot** completely understand the ways of God nor His workings in an individual life.

Romans 2:1-4 says, *"Therefore thou art inexcusable, O man, whosoever thou art that judgest: for wherein thou judgest another, thou condemnest thyself; **for thou that judgest doest the same things.** But we are sure that the judgment of God is according to truth against them which commit such things. And thinkest thou this, O man, that judgest them which do such things, and doest the same, that thou shalt escape the judgment of God? Or despisest thou the riches of his goodness and forbearance and longsuffering; not knowing that the goodness of God leadeth thee to repentance?"* (Emphasis mine.)

These verses have been a real challenge to me in my attitude toward divorce. I have done a lot of marriage counseling and, though I try to be what I ought to be as a wife, I have never counseled any wife who is failing in her marriage whose failures I have not also committed in my own marriage. Perhaps I haven't failed to the same degree, but I contend that the actions — or at least the attitudes — that cause divorce are a part of every marriage at some time.

If you are still married to your original spouse, **congratulations!** You truly have obeyed a very important command in the Bible. However, your marriage is not still together because you are a good wife. It is still together because of the mercy of God! I cannot judge the divorced because, at some time in my life, I have done some of the same wrong things which caused their divorces.

It always breaks my heart to hear of a divorce. I am a writer and a teacher mainly on the subject of marriage. I believe in the sanctity of marriage, and I do not believe in divorce. I never like to see a wounded marriage die.

When a person like myself hears of a divorce, it is easy to try to find a reason for it. It is easy to try to explain what the wife did wrong to cause the husband to forsake her. Why? It's because I tend to think that if I can find an explanation, I can prevent this from happening in my own marriage; but this is judging, and judging is wrong. No one knows why any marriage fails unless that person is one of the spouses involved. No one completely understands the workings of God in the life of another person. It is sometimes hard enough to understand His workings in our own lives.

When I judge the divorced, what am I really judging? The Bible says that when I judge another, I am really **despising** the goodness of God, as well as His longsuffering and forbearance. I am despising the same goodness of God which has kept my marriage together and has led me to repentance from my own unrighteous deeds. Let's put it more bluntly: When I judge the divorced, I am despising God!!

Though I hate divorce and I teach that I hate divorce, I have a message in this chapter for every divorced person. The message is, "I love you, and if I have ever judged you wrongly, I am sorry!"

4. **The separated woman should cry out to the Lord to meet her needs and the needs of her children if she has them.**

5. **The Lord hears the cries of children of divorce.** The world would try to tell us that divorce does not hurt America's children. This is untrue! Tragic is the hurt and loneliness which comes to the children of divorce. Yet how comforting to the single mother to realize that God hears their cry. What a comfort this is to those little children who are forsaken by a parent. My wish is that every Christian would be as compassionate as the Lord Jesus to hear the cry of children of divorce.

6. **God comforts the forsaken wife.**

7. **God desires the forsaken wife to tell Him exactly how she feels.**

8. **God has promises for the children of divorce, especially when their parents seek His face.**

9. **God has provisions for the single mother and for the children of divorce.**

10. **God is with the children of divorce and with their parents in spite of their failures and disappointments.**

11. **God will make of the single mother and of her children something useful.** Ishmael grew, was married and became the head of a nation. Perhaps those scarred by divorce cannot be exactly as they would have been, but it is very possible that God has great plans for them, especially as they seek Him and obey Him.

It is especially sweet to me that God made Ishmael an archer. Ishmael learned a typically masculine trade and sport. This can remind the single mother that it is possible for her to be both mother and father if she has to and it is possible, with God's help, for her to rear a son who is masculine.

12. **The single mother must not run away from her responsibilities.** God told Hagar to pick up the child, Ishmael, and to hold him in her arms. When Hagar did this, God then began to provide for them. Many are the single mothers who wish to flee the responsibilities of motherhood. Perhaps they seek to flee the responsibilities of any relationship at all. I can only imagine how heavy the burden of child rearing must be without the strength of a husband. I can only imagine how heavy every responsibility must be to the divorcee. May this chapter be one of encouragement to you. This was God's message to Hagar. This is God's message to you:

"God sees you."
"God hears you."
"God is with you."
"Pick up the child."
"Pick up your burdens."
"God will provide for you and yours."
"Carry on."

Rebekah —
A Lesson on Priorities

❦

*"And Isaac brought her into his mother Sarah's tent,
and took Rebekah, and she became his wife;
and he loved her: and Isaac was comforted
after his mother's death."*
(Genesis 24:67)

Chapter 6
Rebekah
Genesis 24

$\mathcal{I}$N THE BEAUTIFUL LOVE story about Isaac and Rebekah, we learn about the blessing God bestows upon parents who follow Him. We also learn about the blessings God bestows upon the submissive wife. I have done a lot of studying, reading, counseling and teaching on the subject of marriage and the Christian family. It seems that the longer I work with married couples, the more I am convinced that submission on the part of the wife is the key to a successful marriage and to successful child rearing. In fact, I would say the ultimate child-rearing tool is submission.

Rebekah had a mother-in-law, Sarah, who was a follower and a submissive wife in spite of her many weaknesses. Abraham followed God, Sarah followed Abraham and God gave them an obedient son who even let them pick out his wife sight unseen. God also gave them an obedient servant who took a long journey, following instructions completely until he found the woman God had chosen for Isaac's wife. God carried on the tradition of obedience by giving Isaac an obedient wife who listened to the Holy Spirit of God well enough to know exactly what to do when confronted with Abraham's servant at the well.

Abraham told his servant to return to Abraham's homeland to find a bride for Isaac. Abraham's servant prayed and asked the Holy Spirit to lead him, which is always the proper way to go about finding a spouse. The servant asked the Holy Spirit to let him know that he had found the right girl for Isaac by sending her to a certain well and by leading her to offer drink not only to the servant, but also to his camels. God answered the servant's prayer by sending Rebekah to the well and by causing her to offer to provide drink for him and his camels.

What a hard worker Rebekah must have been! To provide drink for the camels of Abraham's servant and his entourage was a lot of work. Each pot of water had to be drawn from the well and probably carried on Rebekah's head to the camel. It would take several pots to quench the thirst of even one camel. Yet Rebekah was hospitable enough to offer to do this task. God certainly must put priority upon the quality of being a hard worker when He leads a young man to a wife. Part of being a godly wife and of being a good candidate for marriage is to learn to work hard. When it comes to finding the right spouse, character and the qualities of being a hard worker are sorely overlooked in this day and age; but God does not overlook them.

One of the sweetest phrases in the Bible is found in Genesis 24:27b where it says, *"I being in the way, the LORD led me."* If the servant had not been obedient to God and to Abraham by going to the place where he was supposed to go, he would not have found God's choice. Again, obedience seems to be the key to the happy ending of this beautiful love story. People who want to make the right choices in life, people who wish to meet God's choice for a marriage partner, must go to the places where God leads them. They must also stay away from the places where God would not have them to go. We must be where we ought to be in order to find God's will for our lives.

After Rebekah had met the prerequisites for being Isaac's bride, the servant told her about Abraham, Isaac and about his prayer to God to find a wife for Isaac. The servant presented Rebekah with a golden earring and with two golden bracelets and then asked permission to stay in Rebekah's home. Her answer was positive and hospitable, which reminds us of another good quality for a godly wife.

Rebekah ran home and told her family about what had happened at the well, and her family greeted the servant hospitably as well. This must have been a godly family for it seems that they immediately recognized the workings of God in this situation. They were willing to make a supreme sacrifice by sending their daughter into a far away land to become the wife of God's choice for her, a man whom they had never met or seen. Their response to Abraham's servant is found in Genesis 24:50 and 51: *"The thing proceedeth from the LORD: we cannot speak unto thee bad or good. Behold, Rebekah is before thee, take her, and go, and let her be thy master's son's wife, as the LORD hath spoken."*

Understandably, Rebekah's family wished her to linger for a while so that they could enjoy a few last days together. Abraham's servant, however, was in a hurry to get back to his master with news of his success in finding Isaac's bride. The parents left the decision about whether to leave immediately up to Rebekah. In spite of Rebekah's loneliness for her family, she was anxious to follow God's will and to become what God wanted her to be — Isaac's wife. She decided to leave right away. Abraham's servant and his men and Rebekah and her maids left immediately for the long journey.

The Bible tells us that Isaac was walking in the fields when Rebekah arrived. She could see him far off. Rebekah jumped off of her camel and asked the servant the identity of the man walking in the field. Rebekah covered herself with a veil, and Abraham's servant told Isaac about the preceding events. This love story is ended (or should I say begun?) with a beautiful verse in Genesis 24:67, *"And Isaac brought her into his mother Sarah's tent, and took Rebekah, and she became his wife; and he loved her:* **and Isaac was comforted after his mother's death**.*"* (Emphasis mine.)

I believe that I — like Isaac — married not just a good spouse, but **the** spouse which God divinely chose for me. I can identify with this verse very well, for I know how uniquely special is the love between two people whom God has placed together. I know what a comfort the love of God in marriage can be. The priority for Rebekah's life must truly have been to comfort Isaac, the man to which God had so obviously led her. This was a priority which Rebekah cared for with success . . . until she became confused about her priorities.

It was many years before Rebekah was able to bear children. She was barren, but after a long wait and probably many years of comforting her husband, Isaac's prayer was answered. Twins were conceived in Rebekah's womb.

Every mother remembers the joy of feeling that first kick from the child moving inside her. As the day of birth approaches, every mother feels extreme movement from the child within her body and some discomfort. But Rebekah must have felt some extreme discomfort as the Bible says that *"the children struggled together within her."* (Genesis 25:22) Rebekah asked the Lord why it was so, and He told Rebekah that two nations were being born in her womb. Shortly thereafter, Jacob and Esau were born. Though Esau came first and was the stronger of the two babies, Jacob was the most blessed of God. So began two great nations; and so began, it seems, the confusion of Rebekah's priorities.

Rebekah, who had been such a comfort to Isaac, became especially fond of one of those babies. So fond was she of Jacob, the "mama's boy," that she tricked her own husband (the one for whom God specially handpicked her) into giving Jacob his blessing. Rebekah stole from her son, Esau, what was rightfully his. Rebekah's favoritism backfired as she lost what was dearest to her. Jacob had to leave Rebekah and his home to escape Esau and his desire to murder his brother.

What Rebekah did is unthinkable to me. When I think of the love that I have for my own husband, it is difficult to imagine deceiving him in such an enormous way at such a vulnerable time in his life. When I think of the love that I have for my own two children, it is difficult to imagine stealing from my firstborn something so important and rightfully hers.

But Rebekah was not a bad lady. We've already discussed some wonderful qualities which she possessed. She was hospitable, hard-working and obedient. Rebekah seems to have been a good lady who, at the end of her life and her marriage, acted in a very bad way. What do I believe was the reason for the change in Rebekah's life? I believe the cause was mixed-up priorities. When a person's priorities are out of order, that person can change from a great Christian to a mediocre or even a bad Christian. When a good marriage has its priorities out of order, the marriage can change to a mediocre or even a bad marriage. Allow me to share with you some of the things that can be learned about priorities from the life of Rebekah.

1. **A woman's number one priority aside from her walk with God is to comfort her husband**. We see the importance of a husband in a wife's life as we read about Rebekah leaving her entire family on the spur of the moment because she felt God would have her to marry a man she had never met. A woman's husband should definitely come before her parents and should be her first priority.

Though a woman's **role** in the marriage is the role of submission, a woman's main **duty** in a marriage is to comfort or to encourage her husband. Other than perhaps praying for her husband, I cannot think of any other task performed in marriage that can be a greater blessing to a man and to the marriage relationship itself.

Of course, a woman can be a great comfort and help to her husband by keeping his house clean and lovely, his clothes clean and his meals cooked; but a deficiency in these areas can be overlooked when a man has a wife who is an encouragement to him. On the other hand, a wife who is an efficient homemaker but who fails to be an encouragement to her husband pleases her husband very little.

There is more than one way to comfort or encourage your husband. Affectionate touch, admiring words and loving smiles are all important parts of comforting one's husband. However it is applied, a woman's priority in being a wife is to comfort her husband. It is almost a natural instinct for the unmarried sweetheart to provide constant encouragement when she is with her beau. However, the married woman often becomes the total opposite of an encouragement. The most dramatic change in this area occurs when a wife becomes a mother, and that leads us to my second point.

2. **A woman should remember that her number two priority is rearing children, and this priority should *never* become number one in her life**. Rebekah was a comfort to her husband until precious little Jacob came along. She probably felt Isaac was a man who enjoyed hunting and rough, masculine things. Rebekah might have thought he just could not understand Jacob like she could. Isaac seemed to have so much in common with Esau. They shared so much together, but she believed Jacob really needed her.

So often, a wife is a comfort to her husband until a baby comes. The baby becomes the apple of his mother's eye. One so small and helpless really does need the comfort of his mother, after all. The husband just can't compete with the cuteness and the dependency of a precious baby.

One of the things which surprised me when I became a mother was how quickly my baby daughter, Jaclynn, worked her way into my heart. I knew that I would love her, but I did not realize that she would find her way into a place in my heart which had been previously set aside for my husband, Jack. I had no idea the love I had for a one-year-old baby girl could try to take the place of that which I had for a grown, 24-year-old man. But it could have if I had allowed it to.

I was very fortunate to have parents and other wise adults to teach me about priorities. In fact, the very day that I went into labor with Jaclynn, I heard my pastor father preach a sermon on putting your husband before your children. (Let me say that he had no idea that I was in labor at this time!) Whenever I have felt my heart being taken away from my husband by my children, I have done something to change my heart. The following are some of the things I did and still do:

A. I go on weekly, scheduled dates with my husband.

B. I do not allow my children to sit between my husband and me in the car, in church, etc.

C. I remained faithful to church services by using church nurseries when my children were small. I enjoyed sitting beside my husband as much and almost as often after my children were born as I did before they were born.

D. I do thoughtful things for my husband, and this was especially true when my children were babies.

E. I remind my children often that their father is first in our home and in my life. I turn my children's hearts toward their father. I decided long ago that I **wanted** to take second place in their lives.

These are just a few ideas, but they will help you tremendously as you strive to keep your husband as your first priority.

3. **Each individual child should have the *same* priority in a woman's life**. Though I love my own two children in very different ways, I remind them often about my love for **both** children. One is a girl and one is a boy, so they play very different roles in my life. Yet, I strive to love them equally and to treat them both with fairness.

Let me close this chapter by reminding you that I do not believe Rebekah was a bad lady. I believe that she was a lady who had a sensitive walk with God and who possessed spiritual greatness. God in His mercy used Rebekah to rear a prince of Israel. Yet, Rebekah's life probably ended with great sorrow. Why? Her priorities were out of order. When Rebekah gave one child priority over the other, she lost **both** of her children. Esau became an enraged, would-be murderer who most likely felt a lot of hostility toward his mother. Jacob had to flee Esau's wrath by leaving home and going to a far away land. Isaac, the one whom Rebekah was supposed to comfort, probably lost his trust in Rebekah and spent his last days in disappointment and sorrow. The golden years of their marriage were probably tainted. I believe it was all because a great lady had some bad priorities.

May the Christian wives and mothers of today possess the great spiritual qualities which Rebekah possessed. May we follow the leading of the Holy Spirit as completely as she did in her youth. May we also remember our first priority, that of being a comfort and an encouragement to our husbands.

Rachel and Leah —
A Lesson on Jealousy

"Charity suffereth long, and is kind;
charity envieth not; charity vaunteth not itself,
is not puffed up."
(I Corinthians 13:4)

Chapter 7
Rachel and Leah
Genesis 29, 30

W E DISCUSSED IN THE last chapter the awful results of Rebekah's favoritism toward Jacob. Her favoritism led to deception which led to Jacob's having to leave home. Jacob found his retreat at this time in the home of Laban, his uncle. The first person to greet Jacob there was Laban's youngest daughter, Rachel. Rachel was probably a hard worker because the Bible tells us that she shepherded her father's sheep. The Bible also tells us that Rachel was beautiful. We read in Genesis that Jacob wept upon seeing Rachel, causing me to wonder if this was perhaps a story of "love at first sight." We **know** that eventually Jacob grew to love his cousin, Rachel.

There were not any laws at this time about cousins marrying each other, so Jacob asked for Rachel's hand in marriage. When this story took place, it was customary for a man to offer a dowry when he asked for a woman to be his wife. Because Jacob had no dowry to offer, he offered to serve Rachel's father, Laban, for seven years in exchange for the chance to marry Rachel. Laban agreed, and his agreement is followed with one of the sweetest verses in the Bible. Genesis 29:20 says, *"And Jacob served seven years for Rachel; and they seemed unto him but a few days, for the love he had to her."* In that short verse, we read what should be a description of every Christian's feelings about his service for Christ; it should also be the description of every wife's feelings about her service for her husband.

When Jacob's seven years were ended, he married a woman he thought was Rachel. Because women in those days wore a veil to cover themselves until the marriage had been consummated, Jacob had no idea until the next morning that he had really married Leah, Rachel's older sister. Laban gave some excuse about the oldest daughter being required to be given in marriage first. However, historians tell us that there really was no such law at that time. It is unclear exactly why Laban tricked Jacob as he did. Perhaps he was enjoying the free labor he received from Jacob and desired to negotiate another seven-year contract.

Regardless of Laban's reasoning, Jacob got what he deserved. He reaped what he had sown and, in Jacob's life, Rebekah reaped what **she** had sown. Both Jacob and Rebekah had been deceitful, and Jacob was deceived in a very ungodly and cruel way. After Jacob and Leah had been married for a week, Jacob also married Rachel in exchange for another seven years of service to Laban.

In the Old Testament days, God winked at the ignorance of men. He permitted polygamy, but it has always been God's plan for one man to be joined in marriage to only one woman. In the union between Jacob and Leah and Rachel, we see the detriment of polygamy — jealousy. Both women shared the same husband and, as a result, they envied each other for the rest of their lives. They made many, if not all, of their decisions of life based on that envy.

In the 1990's, many people, even God's people, are swallowing the devil's lie that divorce can be amicable and can improve a person's life. Though I believe that God loves divorced people and will use them and bless them again, I do not believe that it is ever God's perfect plan for a man or a woman to have more than one living spouse in a lifetime. It takes a long time to rebuild a life after divorce, and there are many disadvantages with which people must contend. One of those disadvantages is the envy which exists between divorced people and their new spouses and ex-spouses.

Jacob favored beautiful Rachel, and God showed his compassion for the underdog by blessing Leah with children first. In fact, God blessed Leah with four sons and still Rachel had not conceived. I believe that Leah must have been a godly Christian, in some ways more godly than Rachel. I think that Leah's more plain appearance perhaps caused her to seek God more. Her devotion to her God is manifested by the names which Leah gave to her four sons. All four names — Reuben, Simeon, Levi and Judah — have meanings which reflect Leah's desire to win the affection of her husband and of her desire to praise and worship God. Truly Leah desired the acceptance and the affection of her husband. The rejection which she felt caused her to turn to God, and God did not leave Leah forsaken.

While Leah was bearing sons and praising God for it, Rachel was being consumed with jealousy. Rachel was so jealous that she became consumed with having children. Rachel wanted children not so much because she wanted to glorify the Lord and honor her husband, but because she wanted children in order to compete with Leah. Rachel's competitive nature caused her to blame Jacob for her childlessness. Jacob became weary with Rachel's complaining and exhorted her to remember that he was not God. As any Christian husband should, Jacob tried to get Rachel to seek the Lord in her grief.

It is hard to trust God, however, when one is possessed with jealousy; instead, Rachel handled her grief another way. She gave her handmaid, Bilhah, to Jacob so that he might commit adultery with her. In that way, Rachel was imitating her grandmother, Sarah; and the sin committed two generations beforehand was passed down. Bilhah bore two sons, and Rachel named them. The first son was named Dan to show that God had judged in Rachel's favor. How often Christians commit sin in the "name of God." We say He led us to do things which we know are against the Bible. We claim the victorious Christian life when we know in our hearts there is no victory when God's principles are being violated. Rachel named Bilhah's second son Naphtali, which reflects Rachel's obsession with jealousy. *Naphtali* basically means *I have wrestled with my sister, and I have won.*

When Leah saw the extremes to which her sister would go to hurt her, she foolishly chose to compete also. Leah had stopped bearing children, so she gave to Jacob **her** handmaid, Zilpah. Two more sons were born, Gad and Asher.

These two sisters were so competitive that they fought over mandrakes which Jacob's firstborn, Reuben, had brought in from the field. The root of the flowering mandrake was believed to promote fertility, and Rachel envied even the simple act of a little boy bringing flowers to his mother. Rachel told Leah that she could have Jacob in **her** bedroom for the night if she would give Rachel the mandrakes which Reuben had brought her. The deal was made. Jacob went in unto Leah, and Leah conceived again. God's favor did what the mandrakes and superstition could not. Leah bore two more sons, Issachar and Zebulun, and a daughter, Dinah.

In spite of her sinful attitude and the bad choices she had made, God remembered Rachel and finally gave her a son of her own womb. Rachel named him Joseph. How thankful I am to God that He remembers that we are dust and blesses us so often in spite of ourselves.

These women were not heathen and ungodly women. In fact, when Jacob came to the point where he felt it was time to go home, neither Leah nor Rachel tried to dissuade him from taking them away from their family. Both women said, *"Whatsoever God hath said unto thee, do."* (Genesis 31:16b) With the support of his wives, Jacob left Laban and began his journey home. On the way home, Rachel gave birth to another son and died in childbirth. Before she died, Rachel named him *Ben-o-ni* which means *son of sorrow.* Jacob renamed him *Benjamin* which means *son of my right hand.* He did not wish to be reminded of the sorrow of losing Rachel every time he called his son's name. Truly Jacob loved Rachel. It was her two sons who would remain Jacob's favorites for the rest of his life. This favoritism would cause much grief to Jacob's family, but it was nevertheless a testimony of Jacob's enduring love for Rachel.

When Rachel died, a long-lasting feud between two sisters died also. This feud was based on jealousy and envy. God, in His mercy, allowed a great nation to be born from these twelve sons who were conceived more out of competition than out of love. One of those sons was Joseph who was, I believe, one of the cleanest and finest Christian men in the Bible. Yet many bad choices were made by these two women, and much sorrow was endured because of their jealousy. To avoid this happening in our own lives as wives and mothers, allow me to share with you some lessons on jealousy:

1. **We must realize that divorce and remarriage are never in God's perfect plan and will bring upon us more problems than they solve, one of those problems being jealousy**.

2. **We must realize that jealousy stems from vanity and pride**. We must not overemphasize the outward appearance or lean upon it for our help as so many women do. It was probably Rachel's great beauty which caused her to depend upon God less and upon her own scheming more.

3. **We must realize that jealousy is never satisfied**. Rachel was already more favored by Jacob. I am not sure that any man in history loved a woman as much as Jacob loved Rachel. This did not satisfy Rachel, however, because **her** love was based on jealousy. A wife will often strive to get her husband's attention because she is afraid someone else will have it. She seeks her husband's attention as a way of fulfilling her own vanity and pride. If the love in a marriage is based on jealousy, when the jealousy is gone, the love will be gone.

4. **We must realize that we must not meddle with jealousy**. Proverbs 29:9 tells us that *"If a wise man contendeth with a foolish man, whether he rage or laugh, there is no rest."*

Jealousy is a common emotion between women, and it is a foolish emotion. A wise woman will not involve herself with the petty jealousies which crop up among women. This is especially good advice for a woman who works with or lives among many women. If a woman notices jealous words or deeds being hurled her way, she should not retaliate as Leah did. She should remove herself from the situation if she can, and she should handle the jealousy by trusting the Lord. A jealous woman is one with whom she should not contend.

5. **We should realize that jealousy causes us to blame others when the real problem lies within our own hearts**. What peace Rachel could have had in her marriage if she had accepted her lot in life rather than blaming her husband.

6. **We should realize that jealousy clouds our minds and causes us to make bad choices and to lose our faith in God**.

7. **We must realize that jealousy causes us to find displeasure even in the small delights of others**. It takes away our pleasure. Rachel found jealousy rather than pleasure in the simple act of a small boy bringing flowers to his mother.

How can we avoid jealousy?

A. By trusting God rather than things such as appearance and talent for our identities as wives and mothers. We must constantly be learning about our worth to God and enhancing the beauty of our inward spirits by walking with Him.

B. By accepting the negatives and the weaknesses in our lives (such as childlessness) and trusting God in these.

C. By not comparing our strengths and our weaknesses with the strengths and weaknesses of others.

D. By delighting in the blessings (such as the favor of a husband) and the pleasures which are ours rather than longing for and begrudging the blessings which come to others.

E. By refusing to contend with those who speak jealous words and commit jealous deeds.

I have admitted and will admit again that I have struggled with jealousy in my own life. While enjoying the favor of a wonderful husband during fifteen years of marriage, I have sometimes felt jealous of the other women in his life. When these times come, I simply remember that God did not make me a wife so that I might struggle to keep my husband from noticing some other woman. My responsibility as a wife is to meet my husband's needs. His feelings toward me are between him and God.

When we struggle to keep our husbands, we actually drive them away; and we fail to enjoy the pleasure and delight of the love they do have for us and of all of life which we could be sharing with them. Truly, jealousy is a green-eyed monster which should not be contended with in any of our lives. Yet God in His mercy remembers we are dust and does not forsake us. He blesses us in spite of so many choices which are tainted with the sin of jealousy. What a wonderful God we have! He is to be every woman's total identity, her greatest pleasure and delight.

Potiphar's Wife — A Lesson on Purity

❦

"None that go unto her return again,
neither take they hold of the paths of life."
(Proverbs 2:19)

Chapter 8
Potiphar's Wife
Genesis 39:7 -21

M Y FAVORITE BIBLE CHARACTER is probably Joseph. Very few Bible men have as clean a testimony as Joseph does. His testimony and his purity, however, cost him a few years of freedom.

Joseph was working as a slave for a man named Potiphar. Potiphar was captain of Pharaoh's guard. Potiphar was so impressed with Joseph that he eventually placed him over his entire house and everything he had. This placed Joseph in an awkward situation. He was at home with Potiphar's wife, perhaps alone, when Potiphar was not there. During the years my husband and I have done marriage counseling, I have learned that it is not a good idea for a man to spend time alone with a woman who is not his wife, even if he trusts himself and the woman. Even if Joseph was not alone with Potiphar's wife, he still was in a familiar home surrounding with a woman who wasn't his wife day after day; and this is also unwise. Because Joseph was a slave, I doubt very seriously if Joseph had a choice in the matter. Nevertheless, it was an awkward situation.

The Bible says that Potiphar's wife *"cast her eyes upon Joseph."* (Genesis 39:7) She then asked Joseph to lie with her. Joseph refused by reminding her of the great amount of confidence which her husband had placed in him. Potiphar had shared everything with Joseph except his wife. Joseph could not take what was not rightfully his. Joseph asked her this question, *"How then can I do this great wickedness, and sin against God?"* (Genesis 39:9c)

Potiphar's wife was persistent, and every day she asked Joseph to lie with her. When she could not get him to do so, she asked Joseph just to be with her. Joseph knew that it all meant trouble, so he continued to refuse. Finally, Potiphar's wife grabbed Joseph and tried to entice him physically. When she did so, Joseph did what every wise man does when he is enticed by any woman who is not his wife — he ran. He accidentally lost his garment at this time and was so determined to get away that he simply left it without looking back.

Undoubtedly, Potiphar's wife had wounded pride, so she called the other men of the house, Potiphar's other servants, and told them a lie. She accused Joseph of coming to her to lie with her and of running away when she began to cry out for help, leaving his garment in her hand. Potiphar's wife saved Joseph's garment so she could tell her story again when her husband got home. Potiphar believed her and sent Joseph to prison.

This story is unthinkable to me. Yet in my fifteen years in full-time Christian work, my husband and I have counseled with several couples where one or both spouses have been a part of the same type of situation. I have not counseled ladies who have actually sent an innocent man to prison. Yet I **have** talked to wives who have propositioned another woman's husband, and they **have** left these men imprisoned in some way. Proverbs 2:19 tells us that *"None that go unto her return again, neither take they hold of the paths of life."* This verse is telling about the impure woman, and it tells us that **every** man who commits adultery is imprisoned with her for the rest of his life in some way.

I am not trying to condemn these women or their prey. I have counseled ladies who I believe have repented of their sin and gone on to become good Christians, wives and mothers. Yet this verse does teach us that the impure woman's prey will never completely return from his backslidden condition to the useful life in God's perfect will that he could have lived.

I don't know about you, but I don't wish to be responsible for causing someone to forfeit what they could have done for Christ. Neither do I want to forfeit all that God has for me. Because of this, I have tried to learn some lessons on purity from Potiphar's wife. Allow me to share with you some principles on purity which I have learned from her.

1. **If we wish to stay pure, we must learn to stay grateful and contented**. Potiphar's wife was a very rich lady. Her husband was the captain of Pharaoh's guard. She had much for which to be thankful, yet she was discontented. My husband, Jack Schaap, is so much more than I deserve in a husband. It takes an extremely patient man to be the husband of Cindy Schaap. Most of my married life, I have delighted in the greatest gift God has given me other than my salvation, Jack Schaap. When I cease to be contented with my husband and with my lot in life, I have really taken the first step toward immorality.

2. **If we wish to stay pure, we must stay busy**. I wonder if Potiphar's wife's problem was that she was absolutely bored to death. She had servants at her beck and call. I am constantly learning in my Christian life that the difference between the unfaithful wife and the happily married wife is not so much a difference in heart conditions as a difference in habits. My heart is desperately wicked, and that is why I have established habits which protect me from impurity. The greatest Christian you know can easily succumb to temptation if he allows himself to become lazy first.

3. **If we wish to stay pure, we must learn that luxury and position cannot make up for neglect in our marriages**. I do not know that Potiphar neglected his wife, but I do know that she was an unhappy wife in spite of his provision and his position. Many men and women mistakenly believe that because both spouses are happy in their careers or ministries, the marriage can survive on the back burner. This is always untrue, and it is especially untrue for the wife. A wife needs to always

give her marriage the priority which God intended for it to have. Both spouses must realize that a marriage cannot stay clean without care any more than a house or a car can. Happy children, large bank accounts, lovely homes and wardrobes and even church work cannot hold together a neglected marriage. When a marriage has fallen apart morally, both spouses can in some respects never "return again" to God's perfect will for their lives.

4. **If we wish to stay pure, we must learn to be accountable**. Potiphar's wife should not have allowed herself to be in a position where she could proposition Joseph without being noticed by others. Perhaps she should have had more women in the house. Perhaps she should have scheduled more time away from the home, especially when her husband was busy and the servants were there. It might also have been a good idea if Joseph had confided in someone and made himself accountable as soon as he realized Potiphar's wife was propositioning him. Perhaps someone could have been a witness when he faced the prison sentence. Too many Christians are naive in not realizing what a few precautions can do to save marriages and preserve purity.

5. **If we wish to stay pure, we must be careful what we see with our eyes**. Potiphar's wife cast her eyes upon Joseph. A pure wife will not allow her eyes to rest too long upon any man other than her husband. She will look a man in the eyes only and will never stare for any length of time at a man unless she is listening to a song, sermon, etc. A pure wife will not cast her eyes upon evil television programs or romance novels. If you cast your eyes at the wrong thing for very long, you will not remain pure much longer.

A pure wife will also be careful about what she thinks. She will not entertain thoughts of lust toward other men; she will not even be excessive in her thoughts of admiration for men other than those in her family.

6. **If we wish to stay pure, we must recognize temptation right away**. Potiphar's wife was persistent in her

behavior toward Joseph. She should have taken action as soon as she realized her feelings were wrong rather than allowing herself to "play with fire" for a while. We should be like Joseph and run from the temptation without looking back.

7. **If we wish to stay pure, we must not be forward in our behavior**. Potiphar's wife grabbed Joseph and was forward in her behavior. A pure wife will not touch members of the opposite sex except for a handshake or common courtesies. She will stand, sit and speak in such a way that she is not forward toward men other than her husband. A woman will be more likely to stay pure if she remains quiet and dignified in her behavior toward men other than her husband.

8. **If we wish to stay pure, we must realize that the desire to be unfaithful stems from lust and not love**. After Joseph fled from Potiphar's wife, she quickly set about to destroy the one after whom she had sought. Why? Because she never loved Joseph. She just had lust in her heart. I have had women say to me such things as, "I don't think I ever loved my husband in the first place," or "I really believe God intended me to be with the other man all along." The devil can and will try to convince the tempted that what they feel is really love. Temptation to be unfaithful to our marriage vows always stems from selfishness and lust.

9. **If we wish to stay pure, we must realize that dishonesty and stubbornness lead to impurity**. Potiphar's wife was a dishonest woman. She told a lie to her husband and others which was big enough to send an innocent man to jail. A woman who keeps secrets and is dishonest with her husband is more likely to fall morally. It is important for married couples to keep the lines of honest communication open.

Potiphar's wife schemed to put Joseph in prison by angering her husband with a lie. She knew how to use her husband and his emotions to get what she wanted. The Bible says in Proverbs 7:11 that the strange or impure woman is stubborn. A stubborn woman will be more likely to lose her purity.

10. **If we wish to stay pure, we must realize that we hurt God when we are immoral**. Joseph told Potiphar's wife that he could not sin against God by committing such wickedness. A person who fears God and loves God as she should will be more likely to stay pure.

11. **If we wish to stay pure, we must realize how much we hurt others when we are immoral**. As a teacher on marriage at a Bible college, as a marriage counselor and as a preacher's wife and daughter, I am very aware of the damage I could do to the cause of Christ should I stray from my husband and become involved in an immoral relationship. I realize that my straying would not only hinder me, but it would also greatly lessen my husband's effectiveness for the Lord. I pray every day that the Lord will keep my husband and me pure and that we will not do anything which would forfeit our opportunity to do God's perfect will for our lives. If this prayer is answered — and I believe it will be — it will be to the glory of Almighty God Who worketh in us *"both to will and to do of his good pleasure."* (Philippians 2:13)

Jochebed —
A Lesson on Letting Go

"Trust in the LORD with all thine heart;
and lean not unto thine own understanding.
In all thy ways acknowledge him,
and he shall direct thy paths."
(Proverbs 3:5, 6)

Chapter 9
Jochebed
Exodus 2:1-10

Dedicated to my mom,
Beverly Hyles

I CAN'T IMAGINE WHAT it would have been like to have been an expectant mother during the reign of Pharaoh, king of Egypt. He made an edict that all the Jewish boys that would be born should be destroyed at birth. It probably took great courage for Jochebed to even carry her baby to term, thinking that possibly the baby would be born simply to die. Little could Jochebed have known that there lay within her womb the man-child who would be the deliverer from all this cruelty . . . or did she?

Exodus 2:2 tells us that *"when she saw him that he was a goodly child, she hid him three months."* I believe this verse is telling us that Jochebed had some kind of realization that God wanted to use Moses and, therefore, his life was to be preserved by her at all cost. Jochebed's mother must have been close to God to have realized this.

Fortunately, I know all about mothers who walk closely to God. When my sister and I got old enough to drive ourselves to school, we kissed our mother good-bye and left her sitting at the kitchen table reading her Bible every morning. My mother doesn't know this, but one day I found her prayer list and found my name on it. I guess I **thought** my mother probably prayed for me, but I was touched to **know** that she prayed for me. I believe Mom gave me and my siblings to the Lord when we were small. Her close walk with the Lord gave her the assurance that the Lord could do great things with all of our lives and that we were created first of all for Him.

Jochebed not only walked closely enough to the Lord to realize the importance of Moses' birth, but she practiced her faith in the Lord by hiding Moses — probably in some obscure corner of her home — for the first three months of his life. Surely the houses in Egypt were checked from time to time. There most likely were Egyptian guards nearby who listened carefully for the sound of crying babies lest any Jewish male be allowed to live. It must have been an agonizing experience for Jochebed. Yet, she did not abandon her job of mother, even when her safety and comfort were at stake.

When I see how glibly the mothers of the nineties take their calling of motherhood, Jochebed's sense of duty is even more amazing. Babies will be abandoned and even murdered in 1994 for much less reason than Jochebed would have had to abandon or abort hers. Yet, she did what her duty and her faith commanded her to do. God took care of the rest.

I have known a modern-day Jochebed as I have seen my mother stoically stand by her calling of wife and mother when we made it hard for her and when we disappointed her. Through the years, I have sensed in my mother a commitment to be loving and to be there when it was inconvenient, when it was hard, and even when we broke her heart. My mother is committed not only to her marriage and to her children, but she is also committed to her faith in God and to her sense of the duty of motherhood. She has done her best during the most difficult times of our lives, and she has trusted God to do the rest.

Jochebed also did her best in difficult times. There came a time, however, when Jochebed could do no more. She had to leave her beloved Moses to the Lord alone. Praying for wisdom and, perhaps, seeking her husband's counsel, she used her creativity to find a way to save Moses' life. God put it in her heart to place Moses in a tiny ark and to set him in the Nile River. How difficult it must have been for Jochebed to follow God's plans for her son rather than to follow her own. How tested was her faith! Her questions must have been numerous. I'm sure she thought, "What if a crocodile is the first to hear the crying baby or suppose an Egyptian guard hears him? God, are You sure this is what You want me to do?" Yet Jochebed knew what she **must** do. She left the child Moses alone in the river, trusting God to be to him what she could not be.

When I have struggled in my own life, I have sensed the creativity and the courage of my own mother as she has tried to be there for me when she could be; and, more importantly, I have seen her allow me to grow apart from her as I have grown in the Lord. I have seen through her life that there are times when you must commit your children to the Lord and take a giant step back in their lives. Yet, I have also seen that there is never a time to stop loving.

Jochebed's prayers were answered, and her faith in God was rewarded. God sent, of all people, the king's daughter to find the baby. Pharaoh and the daughter of the edict giver helped to rear the one who would eventually deliver His people from Egypt. Surely God has a sense of humor and a sense of justice to have devised such a plan.

Miriam, the baby-sitter and the sister of Moses, was nearby to offer to find a nurse for baby Moses. A Hebrew nurse would be a convenient one to have in rearing this Hebrew baby. So, though Jochebed was never able to reveal her identity as Moses' mother, she **was** able to train her son. I doubt seriously that Jochebed told her son who she was for fear that, in his childish ignorance, he would tell on her. So she stood in the shadows and probably watched somebody else being called "Mommy," but she enjoyed the privilege of caring for Moses and training him to become what he should be.

So like a mother . . . so like **my** mother! She let Dad be the hero of the home. She stood in the shadows doing the mundane tasks of motherhood, like cleaning mounds of supper dishes, while we played with Dad or went off to a youth activity. How hard she worked, how much she loved us, and what she sacrificed every day to be our mother was something we could not understand. We would discover it later, when we were parents. So she stood in the shadows, content to be a part of our lives, content to care for our needs, and content to pray that God would help us to become what we should be.

As I think of what a mother really is, I ask the Lord to make me a mother who walks closely to Him. I ask Him to make me a mother who is committed to the "job of motherhood," committed to the love and hard work which being a mother entails. I ask the Lord to help me to stay present and actively involved in the lives of my children, regardless of the sacrifices involved. I ask Him to help me to do the hardest part of being a mother, especially as my oldest child is becoming an adolescent. I ask for help to stand back and let God do what only He can do in their lives. I want to remember that there is a time to stand back, but there is never a time to stop loving.

"Lord, make me content with my place in the shadows and in the privilege that I have to rear my children and to help them become what You want them to be. Lord, make me a mother like Moses' mother and mine!"

Miriam —
A Lesson on Loyalty

*"Confidence in an unfaithful man
in time of trouble is like a broken tooth,
and a foot out of joint."*
(Proverbs 25:19)

Chapter 10
Miriam
Exodus 15:20, 21; Numbers 12

Dedicated to my sister-in-law, Kristi Lemmen,
who won my husband to the Lord

ONE OF THE MOST amazing stories in the Bible to me is the story of how God delivered the children of Israel from Egyptian bondage. The Pharaohs were hard and evil taskmasters. I'm sure that, time and time again, the children of Israel prayed for deliverance as they went about the difficult chores they were asked to perform daily by their Egyptian masters. The children of Israel had been a rebellious people, and God seemed not to answer their prayers for many years. How many times they must have cried out to God wondering if He had perhaps forsaken them. But God had a deliverer . . .

As I mentioned in the previous chapter, Pharaoh's edict said that all Jewish boys must be killed at birth. This was a harsh judgment from God, but one that I believe the Jews deserved. They had, after all, turned away from God time after time to worship just about any old statue god they found. Yet God in His mercy did not completely forsake His children. He never has and He never will. There were two Hebrew midwives who feared the true and the living God. They would spare the Jewish baby boys whom they had been commanded to kill.

As you know, one of those boys was the baby Moses who

would live three months with his parents in their home and then, for fear of being discovered, would be placed in an ark in the Nile River. Now comes the amazing part! God sent Pharaoh's own daughter to save the deliverer He had chosen. Pharaoh's daughter would have a huge part in saving the Jews! I'm sure the Hebrew people looked everywhere for a sign of deliverance. I doubt, however, that they expected it to come from Pharaoh's daughter. What a wonderful God we have!

Miriam was the older sister of Moses who was sent by her mother to watch over Moses and to see what would become of him. How precious is the protection that can come from an older sibling to a younger one when they are trained in the love of the Lord! Miriam showed her Christian character and her good spiritual training when she reacted to Moses being found by Pharaoh's daughter. Miriam remained calm in the situation and very wisely suggested that she find a Hebrew nurse for this child who was really her younger brother. Thus, in caring for her younger brother and risking her life to do so, Miriam helped to save the deliverer of the Jews. I wish that all family members would be as diligent as Miriam in influencing and protecting their relatives. I wish that all children would throw away sibling rivalry and replace it instead with a desire to protect and to influence their brothers and sisters. Miriam showed that children too can have the wisdom of God in dangerous and important situations when given proper training.

Perhaps Pharaoh's daughter was an only child. If Moses was her only son, then he could have been heir to the throne in Egypt. Yet when Moses grew up, he chose to identify himself with the Hebrew slaves in their poverty rather than with the rich and royal Egyptians. Moses eventually led the children of Israel out of Egypt to see the waters of the Red Sea parted and to miraculously walk across on dry ground. Just as they reached the other side, the Jews were able to watch God destroy Pharaoh and his Egyptian armies in the Red Sea as the water returned to its place.

It was Miriam who led the daughters of Israel in a song of

praise to God after this magnificent experience. She sang, *"Sing ye to the LORD, for he hath triumphed gloriously; the horse and his rider hath he thrown into the sea."* (Genesis 15:21) Miriam knew their deliverance had really come from God and not from her older brother. Miriam was truly a spiritual example to the other women of Israel as she led them in this song of praise. Perhaps Miriam was the one who led in the singing because she was especially thankful to the Lord for giving her the courage many years before to watch over her brother and to care for him. She knew she had a part in the miracle which had just taken place.

Eventually, however, Miriam became disloyal to her younger brother. The Bible tells us that she and Aaron stirred up the people because of Moses' sin, and God punished Miriam for it. Moses did something that he should not have done. He married a woman from a heathen nation, a Cushite woman, who probably was not a believer in the Messiah. It seems to me that Miriam had a right to be angry. After all, Moses **had** done a terrible thing — and Miriam **was** Moses' older sister. Who could there have been better than Miriam and Moses' brother Aaron to straighten him out? Miriam had proven through the years that she had much wisdom and spirituality, and she was a leader among women. Did she not have a right to express her disapproval about what Moses had done?

God evidently did not think so! God appeared in a cloud and reminded Aaron and Miriam how He spoke to Moses face to face. God was verifying Moses' position of spiritual leadership. God smote Miriam with leprosy and would have killed her had not Moses intervened. Miriam had to stay outside the camp for some time until her leprosy was healed. The children of Israel could not continue their journey until Miriam had been healed. There are several lessons in this story which teach us the extent to which God hates disloyalty.

1. **God hates the sin of pride most of all, and disloyalty stems from pride**. God punished Miriam's pride in speaking out against the man of God more than He punished

Moses' sin of marrying a heathen lady. Why? Because pride and disloyalty are sins God hates. In spite of Moses' mistakes, God called Moses the meekest man in all the earth. We show our lack of meekness when we "tattletale" the sins of others and try to turn people against them. No matter how much piosity we display to cover our pride when we discuss the sins of others, it is still pride; and God hates it.

2. **God hates the sin of being disloyal toward a family member.** All too often, we consider it natural for family members to bicker among themselves. If God had considered it natural, I don't believe He would have smitten Miriam with leprosy. I am frequently hurt when I hear people criticize their children, their husbands, their parents and other family members as if it were not a sin at all. People often feel too much liberty to reveal weaknesses and place blame toward family members. Brothers and sisters are notorious for their struggles among themselves, and parents usually respond with statements such as, "Well, you know how brothers and sisters are!"

The story of Miriam and Moses teaches me an important lesson. God hates sibling rivalry! God hates disloyalty even between family members. Be careful, Christian lady, about allowing one family member to criticize another family member in your presence. You may just be trying to help the disgruntled family member, but you are also being disloyal.

We need to spend less time running to psychologists criticizing the members of our "dysfunctional families" and more time pouring out our hearts to God alone Who is the Great Physician. We need to spend our time learning instead some old-fashioned principles like loyalty.

3. **God hates the sin of being disloyal toward the man of God.** Moses was one of the greatest men of God who ever lived. Yet he committed a sin which I think to be a major one. Still, Miriam had no right to become his chief judge. God had not given her the authority to do so. I wonder how many church splits could have been avoided, how many ruined lives could have been spared if there had not been a woman in the

congregation who appointed herself judge to the man of God. Miriam contracted a deadly disease for one rebuke toward the man of God. Surely this should be an effective warning to those women in the church who analyze and critique every decision their pastor makes.

4. **God does not allow even spiritual leaders to practice disloyalty.** Miriam displayed real spirituality and wisdom from her youth. She had a great part in sparing Moses' life. She was a real leader among Christian women. Perhaps if we had compared her record to Moses' record, we would have found no sin as great as that of marrying an unbeliever. Yet God must have considered her pride in judging the man of God and of being disloyal to her brother an equal or greater sin because He punished her severely.

How then should we handle the sin of a friend when it is revealed to us? Most of all, we should overlook it and focus instead on ridding ourselves of our own sins. If the sin is damaging our friend and others, the Bible teaches that we should confront our friend personally with his sin **if we know the sin to be true**. If our friend continues to be a damaging influence, we should discontinue fellowship; but we should not discontinue our love. We should never base our loyalty upon feeling or intuition. Our basis should be fact. The friend with whom we should most quickly discontinue our fellowship is the friend who influences us to be disloyal to others. Most of all, we should pray for our friend faithfully and trust God to work in her life.

I would also like to say that a loyal friend always does what is best for his friend. For example, if I believe or even know that someone **else** is being disloyal to my friend, I will not report it to my friend unless it is absolutely necessary to avoid serious damage. A few times in my life, someone has come to me with a statement such as, "So-and-so is not loyal to your ministry or to your family." Nine times out of ten, I do not believe such statements. Rather, I believe that the person speaking to me is the one who is disloyal. You see, a loyal friend would never cause hurt or division between his friends unless he absolutely had to. To keep from being disloyal, I refuse to believe a friend to be disloyal toward me unless I hear it with my own ears. There have certainly been times when it has been obvious by a person's actions that he is disloyal to my church or family even though nothing has been said directly to me. In cases like this, it has been necessary for me to cool my association with such a person. However, I still believe that friendship should not be ended based on nothing but hearsay.

Loyalty is a difficult lesson; I will be the first to admit that. I look back at my own life and find disloyalty and feel two emotions because of it. I feel shame, and I feel gratitude that God has been merciful to me in my disloyalty. I have a strong desire to learn to be loyal to those I love and to the men of God. Yet, disloyalty cannot always be seen as black and white. It is often gray. We sometimes feel we have a right to be disloyal when that disloyalty might help a disgruntled friend, stop a blatant sin or reverse a decision we believe to be wrong. Still, as a pastor's daughter for 34 years, I have seen time and time again what happens to those who stir up people against the man of God. As an individual observer, I have seen what happens to those who speak out in disloyalty against family and friends. I am grateful for a verse God gave me at a time when I was tempted to be disloyal to a friend:

"Confidence in an unfaithful friend in time of trouble is like a broken tooth, and a foot out of joint." (Proverbs 25:19)

I have felt the shame of my own disloyalty, and I have felt the peace of being loyal when it was difficult. I know the latter to be a far more fulfilling experience.

"I am thankful, dear Lord, for Proverbs 25:19 and for the timing which You used to make this verse speak to my life. Lord, I ask You to please make me loyal; please help me to be faithful to my friends! Amen."

Rahab, the Harlot —
A Lesson on Mercy

❦

"Blessed are the merciful:
for they shall obtain mercy."
(Matthew 5:7)

Chapter 11
Rahab the Harlot
Joshua 2, 6:22 -25

O
F ALL THE WOMEN I have studied for the writing of this book, Rahab stands out in my mind as the one I least looked forward to studying. Surprisingly, she was the one I most enjoyed. I have struggled in my attitude about Rahab the harlot because of the differences between us.

I was reared in church and in a Christian family. I have never tasted alcohol or any kind of tobacco. I have never entered a movie theater or attended any kind of dance. I have never been what I would call immoral in my behavior. In fact, what I would call immoral could be considered very decent when compared to the behavior of women like Rahab the harlot. This clean record from my past leaves me very blessed and happy. It also leaves me a little bit pharisaical and somewhat short on mercy.

My response to harlotry has been a lot like my Grandmother Hyles' response when she heard that my pastor father had won a prostitute to the Lord. She said something like this: "That's good that she got saved, but you didn't talk to her, did you?" So, I entered my study time on Rahab with a few misgivings. However, I came away blessed; and in some respects, I came away changed. Allow me to relate to you some of the story and then to share with you how I was both blessed and changed.

Joshua sent two men to spy out the land of Jericho. While in Jericho, these two spies lodged in the house of Rahab the harlot. The king of Jericho heard that the spies were in the land and sent his men to search them out. It was somehow discovered that the men were in Rahab's house for the search party came there and said, *"Bring forth the men that are come to thee, which are entered into thine house."* (Joshua 2:3b)

Rahab responded with these words: *"There came men unto me, but I wist not whence they were: And it came to pass . . . that the men went out; whither the men went I wot not."* (Joshua 2:4b, 5) Herein lies my first problem with Rahab. She did two things that were unjust. First, she betrayed her own country. However, she knew it was God's plan to take Jericho. Her first allegiance was to God rather than country. Secondly, Rahab told a lie when she said that the men had left and she didn't know where they were.

My first response to this is confusion. How could God use Rahab's lie to spare the spies and to conquer Jericho? Yet when I think of my own efforts to serve the Lord, I realize that even my best works are mixed with human frailties.

While Rahab told the pursuers the spies had left, they were actually hiding under some flax on the roof of Rahab's house. After the king's men left, Rahab told the spies of how word of their God and His power in caring for the Israelites had spread to Jericho. She told what the people's reactions were: (1) *"your terror is fallen upon us,"* (vs. 9) and (2) *"our hearts did melt."* (vs. 11) Rahab also professed her faith in the God of the Israelites in Joshua 2:11 when she said, *"for the LORD your God, he is God in heaven above, and in earth beneath."*

Rahab asked the spies to protect her and her family. This shows her faith in God and her desire to find protection in God's people. This also shows her affection for her family. Rahab's request was just because those who show mercy can expect to find mercy.

Before the spies left, she made a covenant with them. They

made their covenant with caution and conditions. (1) The cord which Rahab would use to help them escape must be left in the window. (2) All those family members whom she desired to escape with her should be brought to her house and remain there during the conquest. (3) If she should betray them, they would be clear of their oath.

Rahab let the spies down the outer wall of the city using a cord tied in her window and told them to go to the mountain until the pursuers were returned. They hid on the mountain for three days as Rahab had advised them and then returned to Joshua.

Rahab and her family escaped the conquest of Jericho. She and her family stayed outside the camp for some time and then became a part of Israel. Rahab's family became great in Israel. Rahab became the wife of Salmon and the mother of Boaz, the husband of Ruth. Boaz is depicted in the Bible as a man of great character. Sweetest of all is the fact that Rahab was part of the genealogy of Jesus Christ. (Matthew 1:1-16)

Here are the lessons which stood out to me as I studied Rahab's life.

1. God knows exactly where deliverance is, even in great danger, and will lead us to that deliverance. The spies undertook a very dangerous mission. I can't imagine being in their place. They were two men in enemy territory, alone in a city completely surrounded by a thick wall of protection. It must have been very hard to get in; it would be difficult to get out. If they were caught, the consequences would certainly be grave. Yet God had an unlikely place and an unlikely person all prepared to care for them even in danger. God provided a friend among many enemies.

As the daughter of the pastor of the world's largest Sunday school and the wife of a preacher, I have endured with my family, and still endure, the attack of enemies. This story strengthens my faith as it assures me that God has deliverance prepared for me when I am facing great danger. It is sweet how

God uses unlikely people like Rahab the harlot to protect us from danger.

2. If we have faith in God, we must be willing to risk our lives to serve Him in great danger. I must be hospitable and helpful to God's people regardless of the consequences. Hebrews 11:31 tells us that Rahab received the spies by faith. Rahab would have been imprisoned and probably killed if she had been caught harboring spies in her home. Even today in America, such an action would cause a person to be convicted of treason. Yet, it was Rahab's faith which caused her to help and to identify with God's people even though she might be killed for it.

My husband teaches that one of the foundational principles for Christian growth is being willing to identify with God's people, whether they are peculiar or not peculiar, whether they are popular or unpopular. As the world grows worse and worse and as Satan's attacks against New Testament churches become more and more prevalent, it becomes increasingly difficult to stand with God's people. More and more Christians are leaving churches because they are tired of fighting. They are joining churches where they can feel more "comfortable." These are often non-soul-winning, non-separated churches which are not fighting the devil.

I have found it hard sometimes to face the battles against the devil which I must face as a member of a separated, soul-winning body of people such as my church, the First Baptist Church of Hammond, Indiana. Yet when I read my Bible and seek the face of the Lord, I am always reminded that I am to identify with the people of God even and especially when times are hard. God can use an unlikely person to care for the people of God when they are in danger. That unlikely person could be me. I certainly would hate to have missed this opportunity because I lacked the faith to identify myself with God's people when it wasn't easy.

Rahab was an encouragement to God's people when they were facing danger. She encouraged the spies by telling them how word had spread through Jericho about the greatness of the God of Israel. She informed the spies about the fear the people of Jericho had toward Israel's God, and she informed them of her own faith in this God, the only true and living God. I want to encourage rather than flee from God's people when they are enduring persecution. I believe God can use my encouragement of God's people in a great way even though I may not know about the results of my encouragement until I reach Heaven.

Not only should I encourage the people of God, but I must realize that protection from the persecution of the world does not come from identifying with the world; it comes from identifying with God's people. Common sense would tell us Rahab would have been safest if she had denied the spies entrance into her home and if she had worked willingly with their pursuers. If she had done that, God would have allowed Rahab to be destroyed with the heathen. Instead, Rahab's life was spared because she chose to risk her life to identify with God and His people.

Common sense (our own flesh) tells us that we would be safer in this dangerous world if we would look like the world, act like the world and keep the Gospel to ourselves; but many Christians will be destroyed by the prince of this world because they lack the faith to identify with God's people.

3. God often uses the very thing we give to others to benefit us. The Bible says that *"whatsoever a man soweth, that shall he also reap."* (Galatians 6:7c) It is sweet to me that the same cord which Rahab used to help the spies escape was used by God as a sign to the spies to help them find and rescue Rahab.

4. God can use us in time of great danger in spite of our past. This is the greatest question I have had about the story of Rahab. How could God use a woman who had lived as wickedly as Rahab to do such a great service and then honor her by placing her in the faith chapter (Hebrews 11) in the Bible? If God can honor such a woman as Rahab, are my efforts to remain pure and spotless from the world in vain? Consider also

Tamar, who was widowed and short-changed, and therefore planned and committed incest with her father-in-law yet is found in the genealogy of Jesus. (See Genesis 38.)

The fact that God forgives and uses those with a wicked past has been hard for me to accept in my life. I fear sin — I fear what it can do to my own life; I fear what it can do to my marriage; I fear what it can do to my children. It is hard for me to face the fact that God loves the sinner . . . but He does; and He expects me to also. He will punish my bitterness toward the sinner just as he will punish the impurity of the harlot.

5. Though God can use us, our sins will follow us for the rest of our lives. In spite of all the good that Rahab did, God still calls her Rahab the harlot in Hebrews chapter 11. God does not warn us about sin because it affects His love for us or because it affects our chances of making it to Heaven. We are all sinners — we are all incapable of earning the love of God or eternity in Heaven. God warns us of sin because it hinders our quality of life on this earth. Though Rahab became a member of a godly nation, became the mother of a wonderful son and became a part of the genealogy of Jesus, she was not chosen to be the mother of Jesus. The mother of Jesus had to be pure. God uses the Rahabs of this world, but He also uses the Marys. So it is not fruitless to keep ourselves spotless from the world. God blesses and uses in a special way those who have kept themselves pure. Anyone who has been close to a person who is struggling to get a life put back together after an excursion into sin can testify that efforts to follow God's commandments are never in vain.

So I, Cindy Schaap, long on pharisaism and short on mercy, have gotten right with the Rahabs of this world. I have found as I have studied her life some truly great blessings. I have found the blessing of being able to love and accept the sinner and the blessing of being able to walk **humbly** with God and among **all** men. I, Cindy Schaap, like Rahab, have gotten right with the Lord.

Deborah and Jael —
A Lesson on Strength

*"Finally, my brethren, be strong in the Lord,
and in the power of his might."*
(Ephesians 6:10)

Chapter 12
Deborah and Jael
Judges 4, 5

*D*EBORAH WAS A PROPHETESS which reveals that she must have had a lot of wisdom. She must have had a close fellowship with the Lord for He is the source of all wisdom. Deborah causes me to think of the old Peanuts cartoons where Lucy sets up her stand and gives advice for 5¢. The Bible tells us that Deborah dwelled underneath a palm tree and that the children of Israel came to her for judgment. She gave the children of Israel counsel and settled their differences. Deborah spent so much time under the palm tree that the children of Israel actually named the tree after Deborah.

Deborah gave advice and judgment at a time when the Jews needed it badly. They had again done evil in the sight of the Lord, and God had allowed them to be sold to Canaan under the reign of King Jabin. The children of Israel were very oppressed under King Jabin. He had an army whose captain was Sisera. Sisera's army stationed soldiers at the gates of the camp where the Jews lived and made everything that the Jews did very difficult. Even the drawing of water could be a horrible experience when the Jewish women had to pass Sisera's soldiers to do so. King Jabin would not allow the Jews to travel, to farm the land on which they lived or to do any type of trading or business among themselves or with the Canaanites. Sisera's soldiers remained at the gates to be sure that these rules were enforced. There was no justice in the way the children of Israel and their problems were handled.

The Jews lived like this for twenty years, then God spoke to a lady who always listened very well to His commandments. He spoke to Deborah because He knew she had the strength of faith to act upon what she heard. God told Deborah to call Barak and to encourage him to gather ten thousand men. Deborah told Barak that God would deliver Sisera and his army into his hand.

But Barak was a little chicken-hearted. He said to Deborah, "I will only go if you will go with me. If you won't go, then I won't go." What a strong woman Deborah must have been! Do you think it was her muscle and her brawn without which Barak felt he could not do? I'm sure not. Barak was surely much safer with his ten thousand soldiers than he was with Deborah. What strength could one female possibly offer to an entire army of men? She could offer strength of spirit. Deborah was so strong in spirit and faith that the bravest men in the nation actually needed her presence and perhaps her encouragement and her moral support with them.

God wasn't too pleased with Barak's lack of courage, so He told Deborah that He would indeed deliver Sisera's army into Barak's hand, but He would not do it through Barak. He would again use a woman.

I'm sure it didn't take long for Captain Sisera to get wind of what was going on among the Israelites. Barak and his army of ten thousand men were soon discovered to be gathered together upon Mount Tabor. Sisera collected quite a bit of equipment and **all** of his army and headed toward the Israelite army, and God said to Deborah, "Today is the day!" Deborah said what every good woman should say to the soldiers of God, "Get going, Barak; you can do it because God will help you!"

Sure enough, God did help him! The Bible says in Joshua 4:15 that *"the LORD discomfited Sisera."* God caused him to feel uncomfortable and confused. It is believed by many that God allowed an act of nature such as a flood to stop Sisera's chariot in its tracks right before the gleaming swords of the Israelite army. Whatever happened, we know that Sisera, for some reason, got off his chariot and ran away. While Sisera was running, Barak defeated Sisera's forsaken army with swords.

Sisera ran to the tent of a man named Heber the Kenite who had been a friend to King Jabin. But Heber wasn't home. The only one there was Heber's wife, Jael, and what could she possibly do as one lone woman to defeat Sisera? She could use what resources she had for the service of God's people, and that is exactly what she did. Jael had the resources of charm and feminine hospitality and, with God's strength, she used them as she could.

She very kindly and sweetly offered Sisera a place to rest. She very kindly and sweetly gave him some cover. She very kindly and sweetly brought him a glass of milk. (I've noticed that if I drink milk late at night, it helps me to sleep. I think Jael had noticed that also.) Then Jael very kindly and sweetly drove a tent nail into Sisera's temples and *"fastened it into the ground."* (Judges 4:21) Afterwards, Jael very kindly and sweetly went to meet Barak and said, "I will show you where Sisera is." So God destroyed Sisera, his entire army and even King Jabin; and he used two women to do the job.

After this great victory, Deborah and Barak sang a duet, a song of praise to God and of tribute to Jael and all those who had part in this miracle. Throughout all of this great story are lessons on the importance of strength.

1. **Strength is not just an important attribute for a man to possess; it is very important for a woman also**. I once heard a great lady describe her pastor's wife as being "one tough lady." She had obviously spoken these words about her pastor's wife with pride, yet I felt it was a rather strange compliment. It seemed to me that "one tough lady" better described a member of a motorcycle gang.

Yet as I have watched my mother during her 35 years of

being the pastor's wife of First Baptist Church, Hammond, Indiana, I have learned that it **is** important for a wife to be both tough and strong. I have learned in my own experience of being a preacher's wife for 15 years that my husband needs me to be strong.

2. **A woman's strength should be in spirit**. I am not fond at all of the new craze for women to lift weights and become strong in body like a man is. While exercise is important for a woman, she should not compete with a man in this area. The Bible tells us in Proverbs 20:29 that *"the glory of young men is their strength."* For the sake of his ego, a man needs to feel that he is strong.

Just as there are times when I need my husband's strong body to unscrew pickle jars and to carry heavy objects, so he needs my emotional strength to be his encouragement and his moral support. Though my husband is strong both in body **and** spirit, God gave him a wife so that she could encourage him to be even stronger. You see, the strongest men are sometimes weak. During those weak times, a husband does not need a wimpy wife to fall apart emotionally or to run away and hide.

3. **A woman should learn when to be weak and when to be strong**. This is one of the hardest things about being a preacher's wife. When my husband is home, he needs me to need him and his strength. When he is out of town, he needs me to be strong. He needs me to unscrew my own pickle jars when he is out of town. He just as badly needs to unscrew them for me when he is in town.

I have seen women take the lead and become strong in situations where it was inappropriate. I have heard women say things like, "The best man for the job is probably a woman." I do not believe this to be true. I have tremendous respect for the male gender, and I readily admit that men possess a strength which I do not. Men tend to be repulsed by women who do not know when to be weak and when to be strong. A truly strong spirit knows when to assert itself as well as when to restrain itself. Deborah asserted her strength by encouraging and giving her moral support to Barak. It was Barak, however, who led the army and wielded the sword.

4. **When a woman is strong in spirit, she creates in her husband a need for her presence**. When a woman is strong during times of trouble and uses her strength in a proper way, to encourage her husband, he learns to trust and to depend upon his wife. He has a hard time succeeding without her. Barak had become so dependent on the wisdom of Deborah that he felt he needed her in battle.

When a woman uses her strength at improper times to challenge her husband's authority, her husband seeks to be independent of her.

5. **A truly strong woman asserts her strength without sacrificing her femininity**. Jael did a very brave and strong thing when she killed Sisera. I don't think I could have done it. You see, I hate the sight of blood — especially when it's coming from someone's head! But what I love most about Jael is that she did what she did while using completely feminine resources. She opened her home and provided a place of rest and a warm snack for a tired soldier. Then she conquered the captain of an army. A woman does not have to become like a man to do great things for the Lord.

6. **A truly strong woman develops her strength from the Lord**. I am actually a very weak woman — both physically and emotionally. Yet I have received much strength from my close relationship with the Lord. Deborah had a very close walk with her Lord. I have no doubt that is where she got her strength. That is the only place where true strength is mustered. Deborah's song of praise in Judges 5 gives testimony that she knew Who gave her strength; it was God and God alone. If a wife is going to be strong for her husband and family, especially during times of trouble, she needs God.

7. **When a woman is strong of spirit during the hard times, she can share in the victory during the good times**. Several tribes in Israel chose not to fight in the battle against

Sisera for one reason or another. I'm sure they regretted it on victory day. But Deborah had no regrets. She did not run away or hide when times were tough. She stayed by the side of God's soldiers, and she offered her positive influence and her moral support. Now she lifted her voice in song in a beautiful duet with Barak.

I, too, want to stay by my preacher husband's side — especially when times are difficult. If I do this, I know that I must daily be developing strength through my fellowship with God. I do not wish to run away and hide or to make wimpy excuses as to why I cannot be strong.

"Lord, make me strong in spirit. May every song of my husband's life be not a solo but a beautiful and harmonious duet sung in praise to You for making us strong and giving us the victory — especially when the battles are the hardest. Amen."

Jephthah's Daughter —
A Lesson on Promises

*"For I have opened my mouth
unto the LORD, and I cannot go back."*
(Judges 11:35b)

Chapter 13
Jephthah's Daughter
Judges 11

GOD USED JEPHTHAH EVEN though he was the son of a harlot whose half brothers hated him and disowned him. Yet he was a man of valor and when it came time for Israel to fight the children of Ammon, Jephthah's brothers sought him out and asked him to be their captain. Jephthah had his brothers promise him that he could be their head if the Lord delivered the children of Ammon into his hand. Jephthah wisely sought the Lord's help before battle, and he made a vow unto the Lord. He promised that the first thing which came through his door after the battle would be sacrificed to God.

Jephthah **did** go to battle and God **did** deliver the children of Ammon into his hand. But the first thing to come through Jephthah's door when he arrived home from battle was Jephthah's daughter. This daughter was Jephthah's only child.

Jephthah tore his clothes and with much anguish told his daughter about his vow. We are reminded of the solemnity of any vow we make to God when we read Jephthah's words to his daughter: *"I have opened my mouth unto the LORD, and I cannot go back."*

Jephthah's daughter's response is both startling and hard to understand. She told her father that if he had made a vow to the Lord, then he had better keep it and do with her what he had vowed to the Lord he would do. This noble and brave daughter asked permission to mourn her virginity for two months and, after those two months were ended, she allowed her father to take her life.

We are reminded in this story of how careful we should be in making our vows to God. It seems senseless for this girl to have lost her young life at the hand of her own father, and it probably was.

Yet I am also reminded of the purpose of a Christian wife. Genesis 2:18 tells us that Eve was made in the Garden of Eden to be a helpmeet to Adam. The first woman was made for the purpose of helping Adam to do what God would have him to do and to be what God would have him to be. Different men are called to do very different things for the Lord. Many are called to surrender their lives to the Lord for full-time Christian service. Some are called to make some unique sacrifices.

Our very purpose as Christian wives is to help our husbands keep their vows and to help them do what God calls them to do. Yet many are the wives who do just the opposite. They are their husbands' main distraction from the vows which they have made. Consider Delilah for example. She distracted Samson from keeping his vow to God, thereby causing him to lose his power and his life. We must understand the seriousness of the vows our husbands make as well as the seriousness of our own.

The story of Jephthah's daughter is a very unique one. Is it really right to offer one's daughter to the Lord? Yet its lessons are profound. Jephthah's daughter valued her father's vow to the Lord more than she valued her life.

I, too, wish to respect the vow which my husband has made to the Lord in surrendering to be a God-called preacher. I want to take seriously the things in my life which would hinder him or distract him from the vow he has made. I want to be a helpmeet who helps him remain faithful to his vow. I want to meet the Lord having kept our promises.

Delilah —
A Lesson on Sincerity

"Let love be without dissimulation (hypocrisy).
Abhor that which is evil;
cleave to that which is good."
(Romans 12:9)

Chapter 14
Delilah
Judges 16:4 -31

*T*HOSE OF YOU WHO have read my book, *A Wife's Purpose,* will probably remember this statement: The devil usually gets to a man through a woman. I believe this to be true after having been a daughter for 34 years to the pastor of the largest church in the world and having seen thousands of people come and go spiritually.

The devil definitely used women to cause Samson to fall spiritually. Samson's heathen wife betrayed him by enticing him through tears to tell her the answer to a riddle he had used to tease the Philistines. Samson responded to his wife's insincerity and disloyalty by killing thirty men and stealing the possessions of these men which he used to pay his bet to the Philistines. Samson's father-in-law gave Samson's wife to another man, thinking that Samson hated her because of her betrayal. Samson reacted to this by using three hundred foxes to set the Philistines' crops on fire and by killing a thousand Philistines.

Still Samson did not learn his lesson and gain control over his passion for the wrong kind of women. Judges chapter 16 tells us an experience Samson had with a harlot where he almost lost his life. If it had not been for Samson's great strength from the Lord, he would have been killed at this time. It was Samson's great strength which caused the Philistines to be so adamant about their efforts to kill him. The devil and the Philistines were obviously aware of Samson's weakness for women, and they used insincere women time and time again to try to destroy him. Delilah was the woman who finally finished him off.

The Bible tells us that Samson loved Delilah. Delilah's love, however, was different. Delilah merely feigned (or faked) love for Samson in order to get what the Philistines had promised her. The deal was that she would receive eleven hundred pieces of silver if she could find out the secret of Samson's great strength.

Delilah begged and pouted to get the correct answer from Samson, but he merely responded with teasing lies. Then Delilah used Samson's love for her in a final effort to get him to tell her his secret. Delilah asked, *"How canst thou say, I love thee, when thine heart is not with me?"* (Judges 16:15) Daily Delilah nagged Samson and questioned his love until the Bible says in Judges 16:17, *"he told her all his heart."* Delilah had won the confidence of Samson to the extent that he opened up and revealed to her all that was inside. This is quite a task for any woman to accomplish with any man as the Bible tells us in Proverbs 20:5, which says, *"Counsel in the heart of man is like deep water; but a man of understanding will draw it out."*

Samson told Delilah that his hair never had been cut and that, if it was, he would certainly lose his strength. Samson did not believe that he could ever be vulnerable. He had forgotten that his strength had come from the Lord, and he had become quite accustomed to making his own independent decisions. When Samson opened up his heart to the wrong kind of woman, however, he became very vulnerable. Samson fell asleep overly confident in his strength and unaware of how vulnerable he really was. When he awoke, his hair had been cut and his strength was gone.

Samson awoke and the Bible says that *"he wist not that the LORD was departed from him."* (Judges 16:20c) This is to me one of the saddest portions in the Bible. The Holy Spirit's power had left Samson, and he didn't even know it. How sad to have known the mighty power of God and then to have lost it!

The Philistines plucked out Samson's eyes and bound him in brass fetters. Samson was a prisoner and a slave. He spent his time grinding in the prison house. The lords of the Philistines were so proud of what they had done that they gathered together and had a party thanking their god Dagon for delivering Samson into their hand. In fact, Samson was the main attraction at the party. The Philistines celebrated their victory by putting Samson between two pillars where they could mock him throughout their celebration.

Samson stood between those pillars and asked a young boy who held his hand to show him where the pillars were so he could lean upon them. While a blind and much humbler Samson held on to the pillars, he began to pray. You see, Samson had finally remembered from whence his strength had come. He asked the Lord God to give him strength just one more time so that he might be avenged of his enemies. Samson's hair had begun to grow again and God allowed Samson to pull down the pillars, thereby destroying himself and all the people in the building with him.

It is precious to me how God remembered Samson and strengthened him one more time, allowing him to be used for God again. It is sobering, however, to realize that even though God did forgive Samson and use him again, He also took Samson's life along with the lives of those Philistines. God does forgive us and use us after we have sinned, but the life lived independently of God and His commandments does lead to destruction. It is so hard and sometimes impossible to fully rebuild a broken life after it has been lived in an unholy way for as long as Samson's had been.

I would have hated to have been Delilah and to have been responsible for not only the spiritual demise of one of God's strongest servants, but also the lives of all those who were in the building he destroyed. I wonder if Delilah lived to regret her insincerity and her greed or if she was one of those in the building who died. Whatever the outcome of Delilah's life, I still wish to learn the following lessons from her insincere love.

1. **A wife who sincerely loves her husband will keep his confidences and his secrets**. Men do not like to be discussed. They may like to hear their wives say to others that they are wonderful or handsome, but men do not like to hear their conversations repeated.

It takes a lot of affection and a lot of praise to get a man to share his heart with another human being. Men, in general, tend to be less communicative than women — even as children. A wise wife will patiently win intimate communication with her husband by being affectionate and by praising him. But when she does this, she must realize how vulnerable her husband is. She must never use these intimacies against her husband. Nor should she reveal the weaknesses of her husband that only she as his wife knows. This will cause her husband to lose his strength in front of his co-workers and followers, as Samson did.

2. **A wife who sincerely loves her husband will not love him selfishly**. Delilah feigned love for Samson for what she could selfishly obtain from him. I am afraid that the women who really love their husbands for any other reason are fewer and farther between than we realize.

I often counsel women who struggle with the problem of jealousy in their marriage. I have struggled with this problem a bit in my own marriage. I sometimes look at another lovely woman who has made my husband's acquaintance, and I wonder if he thinks I am as physically lovely as she is. This kind of thinking is prideful thinking which leads to jealousy.

I tell the women I counsel and I often remind myself that the wife who loves her husband unselfishly will remember that she is not married so that she can have her ego fed or so that she can feel that her husband believes she is the fairest of all. A wife's purpose in marriage is to meet her husband's needs. The by-product of this type of unselfish love is that a husband often begins to cherish and adore his wife as if she were indeed the loveliest woman in the world. The by-product of the selfish love of a jealous wife is just the opposite.

While a woman should attend to the quality of her outward appearance as a way of meeting her husband's needs, she should attend more diligently to the quality and sincerity of her inward love.

3. **A wife who sincerely loves her husband will avoid greed and materialism**. One of the greatest reasons for insincerity and selfishness in marriage is greed and the desire for material things. I constantly struggle, and I do mean struggle, to keep money and other material things in the right perspective in my life. A woman should see her husband as more than her provider. Though a husband is to care for his wife's needs, a woman can destroy her husband's strength and his spiritual power by her greed for gaining more and more materially. Greed often leads to immorality.

4. **A wife who sincerely loves her husband will not scheme to get her own way**. There are five tools a woman often uses to gain from her husband what she wants, materially or otherwise. These tools were used in the story of Delilah and Samson, and they are:

A. Nagging. I have tried in my own marriage to learn what nagging is and to avoid it. Repeated nagging can and probably will cause my husband to *"become weak, and be like any other man."* (Judges 16:17c) I wish for my husband to become all that God would have him to be and to possess God's power. In order to see this come to pass, I must avoid nagging.

B. Charm. The Bible tells us in Proverbs 7:21 that the strange woman "forced" her prey with her flattering words. Many a woman has used insincere praise and a charming personality to get what she wanted from a man — whether it was an immoral relationship or a credit card.

It is fascinating how spellbound a man can be when he is enticed by the charm of a woman. Even God Himself expresses the wonder of *"the way of a man with a maid"* in Proverbs 30:18 and 19. When a woman uses her charm and her praise sincerely to build her husband, all is well and good. However, a woman who uses these same tools insincerely will weaken her husband spiritually.

C. Affection. More than one woman has used her physical love for her husband as a reward or as a punishment. This is what Delilah did. She used her affection to get what she wanted. Affection should be a sincere expression of unselfish love. Any other type of affection will not only weaken a man spiritually, but it may also cause him to wander off into an immoral relationship.

D. Love. Delilah used Samson's love for her against him by saying, *"How canst thou say, I love thee, when thine heart is not with me?"* A wife who loves her husband sincerely will never say, "If you love me, you'll let me." Any dating partner who hears those words should probably run. Any husband who hears those words should probably not fulfill the request.

5. **A wife who sincerely loves her husband will work to keep that love from becoming the insincere love that leads not only to the destruction of her loved one, but also to her own destruction**. As I stated earlier in this chapter, it is very possible that Delilah was present in the building that day when Samson destroyed it. What good could eleven hundred pieces of silver possibly have done her then?

Delilah, I'm sure, was a lovely lady to have attracted the eyes of a man like a Samson. She could have used that loveliness in a sincere and loving way to benefit all those with whom she came in contact. She could have used it to build the life of a husband who would later *"arise up, and call her blessed."* (Proverbs 31:28a) Instead she used it insincerely and for herself . . . and a lovely life became no life at all. May we learn to be sincere in our affection, our charm and our love — in everything we say and do.

Ruth and Naomi —
A Lesson on In-laws

"And Ruth said, Intreat me not to leave thee,
or to return from following after thee:
for whither thou goest, I will go;
and where thou lodgest, I will lodge:
thy people shall be my people, and thy God my God:
Where thou diest, will I die,
and there will I be buried:
the LORD do so to me, and more also,
if ought but death part thee and me."
(Ruth 1:16, 17)

Chapter 15
Ruth and Naomi
Ruth 1 -4

*T*HE MORE I READ and study the Bible, the more I realize that it has the answer to every relationship problem we could encounter and to every other problem for that matter. In my marriage counseling, I find that one of the trickiest relationships to make work successfully is that of the mother-in-law and daughter-in-law relationship. Realizing the omnisciency of God, that He knows everything, I have no doubt that He was fully aware of the problems that would exist in this relationship. I do not believe that it is any accident that God included an entire book of the Bible which deals with a mother-in-law, her daughter-in-law and their relationship.

Naomi followed her husband, Elimelech, into Moab because there was a famine in Beth-lehem-judah. I don't believe it was God's will for them to go to a heathen land in order to seek food, so Naomi probably followed her husband into backsliding. During the ten years spent in Moab, Elimelech died and Naomi's two sons married heathen Moabite girls who were named Ruth and Orpah. Not very long after, both of Naomi's sons died leaving Naomi with two widowed daughters-in-law.

Naomi did not wish to be selfish with her daughters-in-law, though they were just about the only living family she had left. Since she had no more sons for them to marry and was widowed and too old to bear children, she encouraged both girls to return to their families. Both girls must have loved their mother-in-law because they both hesitated to leave her. Perhaps they were both concerned about Naomi's welfare.

Orpah was finally convinced to go back to her family. In doing so, she probably went back to the false religion which was a part of the worship of the Moabite families. Ruth, however, decided to stay with Naomi. She could not be convinced to leave her. I believe that Ruth had become a Christian, and I believe that to be one of the reasons she would not go back to her family. In verse 12 of Ruth 2, Boaz said to Ruth, *"The LORD recompense thy work, and a full reward be given thee of the LORD God of Israel, under whose wings thou art come to trust."* This verse leads me to believe that Ruth was a Christian.

When Naomi and Ruth returned to Beth-lehem-judah, Naomi's friends were shocked by the change in her appearance. They were so shocked that they began to call Naomi by a different name. The name *Naomi* means *pleasant.* Naomi's friends began to call her *Mara* which means *bitter.*

Ruth was a great help to her mother-in-law during her bitter times, and she immediately set out to find a way to provide for herself and for Naomi. God was obviously at work in their lives as He led Ruth to the field of a rich man named Boaz. Ruth asked permission from the servants, then picked up the gleanings in Boaz's fields during barley harvest. When Boaz enquired about Ruth and found out who she was, he told his servants to purposely drop some good barley along with the faulty. Ruth collected a bushel of barley to bring home to Naomi.

Naomi asked where Ruth had gotten the barley, and Ruth said it came from Boaz. Naomi began to praise the Lord for providing a near kinsman for Ruth to marry.

Then Naomi gave Ruth what I, being unaccustomed to the traditions of the day, think were some rather strange instructions. She told Ruth to go into the place where Boaz would be resting after supper and to lie down at his feet. Ruth obeyed the advice of her mother-in-law.

When Boaz awoke and found Ruth there, he was startled. Ruth asked Boaz to cover her with his skirt because he was her near kinsman. Boaz praised Ruth for not going after a young man. Boaz was immediately interested in marrying Ruth because he knew she had a good reputation. *"And now, my daughter, fear not; I will do to thee all that thou requirest: for all the city of my people doth know that thou art a virtuous woman."* (Ruth 3:11)

Boaz asked Ruth to stay the night and then to leave early and quietly so it would not be known that Ruth had been there. Boaz gave Ruth six measures of barley before she returned to tell Naomi how things would turn out. Naomi told Ruth to sit still until she knew what would happen. Naomi knew that Boaz would take care of the matter right away.

There was one kinsman who was nearer of kin than Boaz was, so Boaz checked with him first to see if he would be interested in marrying Ruth. The nearer kinsman told Boaz that he would not be able to marry Ruth, and the men made an agreement that Boaz would be the one to marry her. They showed their agreement before a group of witnesses by exchanging shoes, evidently a custom of the day. The witnesses gave Ruth and Boaz their blessing.

Boaz married Ruth, and Ruth became pregnant. She gave birth to a son and named him *Obed* which means *worshiper.* Naomi and Ruth were truly worshiping the Lord for His leading and for providing this baby. The Bible says that Obed was a restorer of Naomi's life and a nourisher of her old age. I think most grandparents probably understand what that statement means. Not only was Elimelech's family name carried on, but Obed became the grandfather of David and was in the line of Jesus' descendants. (See Matthew 1.) In following the Lord and in caring for her mother-in-law, Ruth started a wonderful heritage. In fact, Naomi says in the book of Ruth that her daughter-in-law was better to her than seven sons.

Allow me to share with you some things I learned from this story about the in-law relationships, particularly the mother-in-law/daughter-in-law relationship.

1. **A daughter-in-law should share her life with her husband's family**. Though the Bible says that a husband is to **leave** his mother and father and to **cleave** unto his wife, there can still be a sweet relationship of sharing between the couple and their in-laws. Of course, there are areas where in-laws should be left out and there are times when a couple should guard their privacy. Still, the daughter-in-law should be willing to share with her in-laws. It is usually the wife who will decide how close the family will be to their in-laws, so she has an added responsibility to be willing to share.

There are five things that Ruth shared with Naomi:

A. Ruth shared her path. *"Whither thou goest, I will go."* Ruth spent time with Naomi, and I believe that a couple should be willing to share some quality time with the in-laws. I believe I have a Biblical responsibility to share some time with my in-laws because of what they have done for my husband.

B. Ruth shared her home. *"Where thou lodgest, I will lodge."* Ruth shared her home with Naomi. Now, I don't believe it is wise for married couples to live with either set of parents. Remember, though, that Ruth and Naomi were widows. I do believe that a daughter-in-law should not be unwilling to open her home to her in-laws. I also believe that a daughter-in-law should be pleased to occasionally visit in the home of her husband's parents.

C. Ruth shared her family and friends. *"Thy people shall be my people."* I admit that sometimes it can be a pain to spend time with your husband's Great-uncle Fred and his ten kids when you as a daughter-in-law do not even know them. My father-in-law has seven brothers and three sisters, and it is difficult to keep even their names straight sometimes. But when Jack Schaap became my husband, his family became my family.

My in-laws are very people oriented, and I am not as much so. In the past, I have sometimes been irritated to arrive at their home ready to visit them only to discover they had some friends around with whom they expected me to visit also. Yet when I studied the life of Ruth, I was convicted about my selfish attitude. You see, if people are friends of my in-laws, they **are** my friends.

D. Ruth shared her religion. *"And thy God my God."* Ruth and Naomi shared the same faith. I believe it is important to marry a godly Christian man with whom you can share your faith. God has given me godly in-laws with whom I can share my faith, and I believe it is important for us to share spiritual things.

Many Christian couples cannot say that they have parents who share their faith. I still think these couples have a responsibility to spend **some** time with their parents as an opportunity to be a Christian testimony. I am sometimes concerned about the attitudes I sense when I talk to Christian couples who say they do not visit one or both sets of parents any longer because they don't wish their children to be around Grandpa's cigarettes.

God has given me Christian parents on both sides, and I realize I am truly blessed. I'm sure I do not understand all of the difficulties which can present themselves when there are unsaved relatives involved. There would be some times when it would not be best to have children around in-laws. I still believe, though, that Christian couples should honor their parents as best as they can — whether or not they are saved and separated. A non-loving, pharisaical attitude can cause a poor testimony. Probably at some time in their relationship, Naomi and Ruth were of different religions; but there was still an obvious love relationship there. This shows me that it is possible to love in-laws with different faiths, different standards, etc. The time spent together may be less frequent, but the attitude should be a loving one.

E. Ruth shared her place of burial. *"Where thou diest, will I die, and there will I be buried . . . if ought but death part thee and me."* Ruth was committed to loving and caring for the needs of her in-laws. This was a lifelong commitment. She didn't intend to love her until Naomi made her mad or until Naomi got old enough to be an inconvenience. If we had this type of commitment among families today, there would be little need for the Social Security program.

2. **A mother-in-law should not *expect* any particular type of treatment from her daughter-in-law**. Any relationship begins to deteriorate when the people involved begin to seek what they want rather than trying to be what their loved ones need. The average mother-in-law pouts and fumes when she does not receive from her children and their spouses the time, the hospitality and the concern she thinks she deserves. It is the daughter-in-law's responsibility to give of her time to her in-laws when it is appropriate for the family. The mother-in-law should not demand it. The relationship will be sweet if both are seeking what the other wants and needs.

3. **Mothers-in-law and daughters-in-law should be affectionate and encouraging to one another**. Naomi kissed Orpah when she said good-bye to her. I believe there should be love and affection among daughters-in-law and mothers-in-law. Many times in the book of Ruth, we find Naomi blessing and praising her daughter-in-law. If more in-laws would praise each other rather than trying to outdo each other, their desire to spend time with each other would be enhanced.

4. **Daughters- and sons-in-law should provide for the needs of their in-laws**. Ruth took it upon herself to provide for Naomi. Married children should check to see if their parents have needs and to see that those needs are filled, especially as the parents grow older or if they are in poor health. We, perhaps, cannot be responsible for every need. Funds might be limited. But we can do what is appropriate and share what we have. Many married children who say they simply cannot afford to even buy a gift for parents at Christmas live in nice houses, drive nice cars, etc. This just simply should not be!

5. **Daughters-in-law should take the advice of their**

mothers-in-law. Ruth took Naomi's advice several times, and sometimes that advice might have been hard to understand. I do not necessarily believe that mothers-in-law should volunteer unwanted advice. I believe that daughters-in-law should be wise enough to seek the advice of their in-laws as well as the advice of other older and wiser people.

6. **Daughters-in-law should allow their children to be close to their grandparents**. I'm not sure it ought to be this way, but it is usually the wife who decides where the family will spend time, especially in the case of the children. At the least, the wife has a strong deciding influence — and most husbands are not willing to tangle with a woman who has made up her mind! A wife should encourage her children to be close to her husband's parents as well as to her own parents. Naomi became the nurse (baby-sitter) to her grandson, Obed.

7. **Daughters-in-law should realize what blessings God has in store for them as they properly relate themselves with their in-laws**. Because of Ruth's commitment to Naomi, she became the wife of a godly and rich man; she also became the mother of a descendant of David and of Jesus Christ.

I have a wonderful relationship with my husband's parents. It is a relationship which has always been important to me. I have a mother-in-law who is a praising and affectionate mother-in-law as well as a wonderful mother and grandmother. I have a godly father-in-law with whom I enjoy talking, especially about spiritual things. I had no idea what blessings God would have in store for me in this wonderful family which I inherited through marriage.

Naomi said that Ruth, her daughter-in-law, was better to her than seven sons. I do not believe my in-laws could say that about me. Their one son is, after all, pretty special to them and to me. Yet I love my in-laws very much and, though I have failed them in some ways, I strive to be what they need in a daughter-in-law. Yes, I love them very much, and you can learn things from Ruth that will increase your love for your in-laws also!

Hannah —
A Lesson on God's Presence

"And she vowed a vow, and said, O LORD of hosts,
if thou wilt indeed look on the affliction
of thine handmaid, and remember me,
and not forget thine handmaid,
but wilt give unto thine handmaid a man child,
then I will give him unto the LORD
all the days of his life."
(I Samuel 1:11)

Chapter 16
Hannah
1 Samuel 1:1 - 2:21

$\mathcal{H}$ANNAH WAS A WOMAN who was loved and cared for by her husband. Though Elkanah had two wives, he was especially partial to the sweet-natured and spiritual Hannah. Yet, Hannah bore a cross. I have learned a little bit about crosses in my Christian life. Crosses sometimes come in the form of an illness or a handicap, but not always. One of the crosses that we are often asked to carry in our Christian lives is the cross of people problems.

Hannah **did** have the handicap of a barren womb, but her cross was compounded by the constant taunting of Elkanah's other wife, Peninnah. Every mother can imagine the pain of being unable to do what a woman finds so fulfilling, bear children. It is hard to imagine being ridiculed about that pain as Hannah was.

Hannah took her pain to the right place — to the altar at church. How many times have I laid my own small crosses at the church altar and found sweet relief. Hannah's bitterness of soul as she left her cross at the altar was so severe that she cried out unto the Lord as if she were drunk. In fact, Eli the priest thought that Hannah **was** drunk.

I relate to Hannah as I recall one afternoon in my kitchen when I cried out to the Lord with such bitterness of soul that I began to cry aloud in agony. It is a good thing that I was alone, because I'm sure I seemed to be drunk or to have been "cracking up." Yet how sweet is the memory of the presence of the Lord which I felt at my altar, the kitchen sink. I cherish that day now, and I am glad I understand a little bit about Hannah's feelings.

The theme of Hannah's prayer was a lot like mine: "Lord, remember me. Lord, notice me." Then Hannah prayed something like this, "If you will give me a son, I will give him back to you."

The preacher, Eli, after he understood the burden which was Hannah's, assured her that God would answer her prayer. I relate with Hannah in that also. Many a Sunday, after episodes of agony and doubt in my own life, I have heard the preacher in my own church as he strengthened my faith through his sermons. He assured me that God was truly able to meet my needs and desires.

Hannah did not just take her cross to the altar, but she left it there and took her pastor's message in its place. The Bible tells us that Hannah left the church with a happy countenance and then ate a good meal. It has been easier for me to take my burdens to the altar than it has been for me to leave them there. Yet I am learning to spend the time outside of my prayer closet praising God with a happy countenance. I give my particular burdens and crosses to the Lord each day during my prayer time, and they are His to carry for the rest of the day.

God came through for Hannah as He has done so many times for me. He gave her that for which she asked — a baby. The baby was a boy, so Hannah could carry on the family name of her loving husband. She named the boy Samuel, which means "asked of God." Hannah did not forget Who had sent her precious gift.

Hannah nursed the baby Samuel until it was time for him to be weaned. Then she kept her promise and paid her debt. She took her son to the place where she had asked for him. Hannah gave him to the One Who had so sweetly answered her prayer and healed the agony of her soul.

I fear if I had been Hannah, I would have griped and wept and, perhaps, really lost my mind when it came time to say good-bye to my baby boy. After all, Hannah had borne the cross of childlessness for so long. She had agonized to see this child born. **This was her child**! But Hannah did not cry this time. Rather, she rejoiced! No matter how much she had agonized to see her dream of childbirth come to reality, Samuel was **not** her child; he was God's.

Hannah was able to rejoice because she had not borne a child for her own selfish purposes as so many women do. She did not ask for a child so that she could feel those chubby hands patting her cheeks. She did not bear a child so that she might have the daily opportunity of watching that child grow. She bore Samuel so that she might give him to God.

Hannah watched over her son from afar. She also went to the temple every year, helping to meet his needs by replacing his outgrown coat from the previous year with a new one she had made with her own hands. Hannah would bear five more children — three sons and two daughters — and Samuel would grow to be a great man of God. Surely God noticed Hannah. Surely He remembered her!

It seems like Hannah's entire life is one great lesson. One does not need to look far to find the truths contained therein. Please allow me to share with you some observations I have made about Hannah's life.

1. **Most of us bear crosses and suffer persecution**.

2. **We should not make too much of our persecutions**. How human Hannah seems as we envision her crying at the altar. The Bible seems to say that Hannah was not just agonizing over her childlessness, but she was also agonizing over the taunting by Peninnah. Peninnah's tauntings were provoking her. Sometimes we Christians are strong and courageous. Sometimes just the criticism or ridicule of another Christian can have us

crumbling inside. Yet even when we overreact to those who have hurt us, God notices our pain. God remembers.

3. **In persecution and in agony, the secret is to turn to the Lord**.

4. **After we have turned to the Lord, the answer to our agony is faith**. We, like Hannah, should go to the church and listen to the preacher when we are in agony. We should believe what the preacher tells us as he strengthens our faith in God's Word.

5. **After we have left our cares with the Lord, we should find comfort and rejoice in that for which we can be thankful**. Hannah had a husband who loved her, and she had the promises of God and of Eli.

6. **When God comes through with His promise, we should remember to praise Him as Hannah did in I Samuel 2:1 and 2**. *"And Hannah prayed, and said, My heart rejoiceth in the LORD, mine horn is exalted in the LORD: my mouth is enlarged over mine enemies; because I rejoice in thy salvation. There is none holy as the LORD: for there is none beside thee: neither is there any rock like our God."*

7. **We should care well for our children as they are answers to prayer received from the Lord**.

8. **We should teach our children to be faithful to church and to worship the Lord at a young age as Hannah did**.

9. **We should teach our children to respect God's man even when he is not perfect**.

The priest of Hannah's day, Eli, had two very wicked sons. (I Samuel 2:12) This did not deter Hannah from taking Samuel to church and from teaching him to respect God's man. Wicked as they were, Eli's sons were in the ministry. Still, Hannah did not become cynical about preachers; instead, she was pleased to have her son in the ministry.

10. **We should rear our children with devotion and with a sense of destiny**. My own two children have been such precious gifts from God. It is sometimes hard to take in all the joy they bring to me. Yet, I must often remind myself that they were not born for my pleasure. My oldest child desires to be a missionary. Her desire may take her away from my husband and me to a remote land. I may someday see her only as often as I would a distant relative. I could think, "Is that fair? . . . She is **my** daughter." Instead, I must remember that she does not belong to me. She is God's. God gave me two children so that I might be able to rejoice at the opportunity of giving them back to Him. In fact, all that God gives me is to be given back to Him. What God may want to do with my children should rest constantly upon my heart as I care for them both physically and spiritually.

11. **We should realize that persecution and bearing crosses teaches us humility and courage**. If Hannah had not agonized at an altar, she would never have had the humility and the courage to give Samuel to the Lord. Her agony prepared her to rear a great man of God. If I had not one day agonized at the kitchen sink over my cross, I could not have the precious memory of the presence of the Lord. His answers to prayer since then could not have been so sweet. I could not have begun to learn the humility and the courage to bear and to do what God has for me.

How well I understand you, Hannah! How well I understand your agony, though ours came in different ways. But what we understand best of all, Hannah, is this: God notices. God remembers.

Abigail –
A Lesson on Peacemakers

❧

"Blessed are the peacemakers:
for they shall be called the children of God."
(Matthew 5:9)

Chapter 17
Abigail
1 Samuel 25

$\mathcal{D}$AVID HAD BEEN HIDING from Saul near the sheep of a very rich man named Nabal. Though David and his mighty men were probably very hungry while away from home and in hiding, they never once looted any of the sheep which belonged to Nabal. Never did they cause any trouble for Nabal's servants. In fact, David and his men had taken it upon themselves to be a help to the servants — probably in sheepshearing. They also provided some protection for the shepherds and their sheep.

It would have been appropriate for Nabal to have repaid David and his men for their help to him because it was the time of sheepshearing. This was a time when feasts and celebrations were held. David, probably realizing this as well as the fact that his men were hungry and in need of provisions, sent some men to ask Nabal if they could have some food. Nabal lived a ways off from where he kept his sheep, so the men set out on their journey.

The Bible says that Nabal was an evil and a churlish man. He responded to the courteous request of David with a bit of sarcasm. He asked, *"Who is David? and who is the son of Jesse?"* (I Samuel 25:10a) Nabal said that a lot of servants part company with their masters. Why should he give food to David?

When David's men returned with the message, David

became angry. He and four hundred of his men girded themselves with swords and went to fight Nabal.

One of Nabal's young workers told Abigail, Nabal's wife, what had happened. He described to Abigail what a help David and his men had been to the servants but he said that Nabal was *"such a son of Belial, that a man cannot speak to him."* (I Samuel 25:17c) Abigail no doubt had heard of David and how he had slain Goliath. She had probably heard the song about Saul slaying his thousands and David his tens of thousands. She knew that her evil husband had picked a fight with the wrong man. She probably also knew that Nabal had committed an injustice by not helping David and his men. After all, Nabal was a very rich man and it would not have been a great sacrifice for him to have paid these men.

Abigail went to work to begin to make up for her husband's lack of spirituality and helpfulness. She took 200 loaves of bread, two bottles of wine, five sheep, five measures of corn, 100 clusters of raisins and 200 cakes of figs. She laid this food on the backs of several donkeys. She sent off her servants with them, and she followed.

When Abigail saw David coming, she got off her donkey and went to David. She fell down before David and asked that the iniquity which Nabal had committed against David be placed upon her. She told David about the food she had brought, and she prophesied that someday David would be anointed king and that all of his enemies would be destroyed. She told David how glad she was that the Lord had used her to prevent David from shedding blood and destroying Nabal. Then she asked David to remember her when he was anointed king.

David decided that there would be no bloodshed, and he thanked Abigail for that. He accepted Abigail's gift and told her to go back to her house in peace. When Abigail returned home, Nabal was holding a feast and he was drunk. In the morning, when Nabal was no longer drunk, Abigail told him what had happened. The Bible says as soon as Nabal heard what Abigail had done *"that his heart died within him, and he became as a stone."* (I Samuel 25:37b) It wasn't until ten days later, however, that Nabal actually died.

When David heard what had happened to Nabal, David praised the Lord for returning Nabal's wickedness upon his own head. He sent his servants to ask Abigail to become his wife. Abigail's response was both enthusiastic and humble. She said, *"Behold, let thine handmaid be a servant to wash the feet of the servants of my lord."* (I Samuel 25:41b) Abigail hurried to David on her donkey, and she soon became his wife. Again, I see so much in Abigail's life which I would like to emulate.

1. **Abigail's good qualities withstood the pressures of evil**. Abigail had been married to a very evil man. I am not sure why. Perhaps her father had married her to Nabal because he was so rich. Many are the parents who seek material wealth as they seek mates for their children. Many are the women who "marry for money" so to speak. Yet it is always wrong to do so.

Abigail means *the joy of my father*. Perhaps at one time Abigail was the joy of her father. Yet, for some reason, she became the wife of a very evil man. However, in spite of Abigail's marriage to such a wicked man, the Bible still says that Abigail was *"of good understanding, and of a beautiful countenance."* (I Samuel 25:3c) These are the types of spiritual qualities that every wife and mother needs, the qualities which endure in spite of the pressures of evil which may surround us in our world today. So great was the spirituality of Abigail that her marriage to an evil man did not affect the beauty of her countenance.

2. **Abigail had a reputation for kindness**. Nabal's young servant boy knew where to go for help. He knew that wise Abigail would reverse the injustice and protect from danger.

3. **Abigail acted quickly and with generosity**. She loaded up the donkeys with food and headed toward David and his men. Perhaps she was afraid of what her chances might be of avoiding the wrath of David, but she did what she could do.

4. **Abigail was willing to defend her husband and to**

take the blame for his mistake. In spite of the fact that Nabal was an evil man and had indeed done something wrong, Abigail did not criticize him. She did not come to David just to watch out for herself. Her concern was also for Nabal. Abigail was committed to her vow to her husband whether he was right or wrong. Her concern was also for David. She did not want him to partake in unnecessary bloodshed.

5. **Abigail had a close relationship with the Lord**. It had to be a close relationship with the Lord which allowed Abigail to prophesy about David's future. She knew that his enemies would be destroyed and that he would someday be anointed king.

6. **Abigail was humble**. It was humility which allowed Abigail to put so much effort into undoing the mistake which her husband had made. Abigail greeted David with humility when she brought him his provision. Abigail responded with humility when David asked her to become his wife. She simply wanted to be David's servant. I am sure that a lot of marriages would be much happier if each marriage partner would enter into marriage with a similar goal.

7. **Abigail was a peacemaker**. This is what I love most about her. Again, Abigail could have just saved her own neck and the necks of those she loved; she could have gone ahead and had Nabal destroyed, but Abigail was a peacemaker. Her main purpose was to make peace and to prevent strife.

In my own life, I have tried to remember the beatitude which says, *"Blessed are the peacemakers."* It is important for a Christian wife to learn the art of peacemaking. A wife, more than anyone else, can get her husband riled up about certain things and about certain people and be a real hindrance to him.

Let me give you an example. Several years ago, one of my husband's fellow workers said something to Jack which was truly hurtful. There exists a sweet spirit among the co-laborers at the college, so I was surprised by what was said — surprised and hurt.

Every wife quickly learns that it is more difficult to see her husband be hurt and criticized than it is to be criticized herself. In fact, to criticize a person's spouse **is** the same as criticizing the person. My first instinct was to run to the college myself and poke out the person's eyeballs. My second instinct was to spend about an hour (at least) discussing with my husband what a "jerk" so-and-so was.

However, I believe in being a peacemaker. I believe in the Biblical concept of living as peaceably as possible among my fellow Christians. I believe in the tremendous amount of influence a wife has upon her husband and, therefore, I believe in the importance of every word a wife speaks to her husband. Because of this, I took a second look at the situation; then I no longer wanted to attack the person who hurt my husband.

I have always admired my husband's ability to get along with all types of people. I admire his ability to handle wrong without retaliating. I chose this time to tell him so. I told Jack that what I admired about him was his being the type of person who would go to college the next day and shake that man's hand as if nothing had ever happened. The next morning as I ironed my husband's shirts, I could picture him walking up and shaking that man's hand; and I indeed felt the significance of those words, *"Blessed are the peacemakers."*

I have not always responded to my husband's people problems (or to my own) as I should. Yet I have worked to be a peacemaker in our marriage. When I criticize another person to someone who is angry, that angry person may feel good for a while. But when he walks away, he will be even angrier, his burden heavier. When I strive to be a peacemaker with the angry person, there may be some initial hurt; but in the long run, I have made his burden lighter.

I am sensitive about people and their feelings — perhaps too sensitive. When I sense hard feelings between people, I often listen for **some** kind word spoken about one by the other. Then I make a beeline to the offended person to repeat the kind words I have heard spoken. Why? Because *"blessed are the* *peacemakers."*

On the other hand, if I hear critical words spoken by one person about another, I try **not** to repeat them. I am so often surprised by the talk which goes on among Christian adults. "So-and-so is not loyal to you." "So-and-so said this negative thing about you." I am not the perfect example of this, but I endeavor to avoid repeating this type of conversation unless I **absolutely** must reveal it. To me, the most disloyal thing a friend can do is to seek to separate his friend from another friend.

Abigail gladly went to become David's wife, and she went in a hurry. She had known the misery of being the wife of an evil man. She had discovered that riches and a nice home could not make a woman as happy as could serving God's man. She gladly chose a home in the wilderness where David hid from Saul rather than the mansion of Nabal. She knew, after all, that it would not be long until she would be the wife of a king. God had told her so!

Abigail had been loyal and had been a peacemaker in whatever situation she found herself. Now she would be the wife of one of God's greatest servants and would someday live in a palace. Abigail's story with its fairy tale ending certainly illustrates the truth and the power behind God's principles, and behind this one in particular — *"Blessed are the peacemakers."*

Michal —
A Lesson on Sarcasm

❦

"And as the ark of the LORD came into the city of
David, Michal Saul's daughter looked through
a window, and saw king David
leaping and dancing before the LORD;
and she despised him in her heart."
(II Samuel 6:16)

Chapter 18
Michal
11 Samuel 6:14 -23

$\mathscr{T}$HE WOMEN OF ISRAEL cried, *"Saul hath slain his thousands, and David his ten thousands."* The Bible says that this chant made King Saul *"very wroth* (very angry), *and the saying displeased him."* (I Samuel 18:7, 8) This saying brought the jealousy to Saul's heart which caused the Spirit of the Lord to depart from him.

The first day Saul heard this saying and from then on, Saul went on an emotional roller-coaster ride where his feelings toward David were concerned. He was obsessed with his jealousy toward David, yet he couldn't quite escape the unconditional love and respect which he so often saw David display toward him.

In I Samuel 18:11, there is record of Saul casting a javelin at David. Two verses later, Saul makes David captain in his army (verse 13). In verse 17 of the same chapter, Saul promised his daughter, Merab, to David. Then in verse 19, Saul changes his mind and gives Merab to marry another man named Adriel.

I hate what jealousy took from Saul and what it does to people today! When I read the results of Saul's jealousy in his own life, as well as in the life of his daughter, Michal, I am more determined than ever to fight this green-eyed monster.

Michal, Saul's other daughter, loved David. Saul was pleased with Michal's feelings toward David because he knew that Michal would be a snare to David. Perhaps Saul understood the character of Michal to be so much like his own that he knew she would be a great hindrance to David. Perhaps he realized what so many parents in the 20th century fail to realize — that the criticism, hatred and jealousy felt by parents has a definite influence on the behavior of their children.

Perhaps Saul also realized what I teach every semester in my Christian Wife class at Hyles-Anderson College. Maybe he realized that the devil uses women more than any other tool to destroy the lives of Christian men. The women the devil uses are not always unsaved and unloving women. Sometimes, they are just critical — like Michal was.

The fact remains that Michal loved David. This is clearly stated in I Samuel 18:20. *"And Michal Saul's daughter loved David: and they told Saul, and the thing pleased him."* The Bible does not say that Michal lusted after David, but that she truly loved him. This teaches me that it is possible for me to genuinely love my husband and still be his worst critic and a snare in his life and service for the Lord.

We are also told in I Samuel 19 that Michal saved David's life on one occasion. Yet, a few pages later in II Samuel 6, we read that Michal despised David in her heart. Her strong negative feelings toward the man whom she had once loved caused Michal to be sarcastic toward him. Therefore, she became the spoilsport on one of the most spiritual and happy occasions of David's life. Michal's spoilsport attitude caused her to receive some severe discipline from the Lord. Her sentence was to have no child unto the day of her death.

I know several women who are unable to bear children. I am sure that God has many reasons for withholding children from a woman. Yet as a mother of two, I cannot imagine the pain of being unable to bear children. To be unable to bear children because of God's will would be one thing, but to be unable to carry children because of some type of punishment would be quite another indeed. I would hate to think my behavior toward my husband would be so awful that it would hinder me from fulfilling the noble calling of motherhood. It saddens me to think that my behavior as a wife might cause God to have to judge me in any way. Because of this, I have studied the behavior of Michal toward David and have discovered the following lessons. Allow me to share them with you.

1. **God judges a wife who is sarcastic toward her husband, especially when her sarcasm is aimed at her husband's service and praise to God**. I hate to say it, but I can relate to Michal's feelings a little bit. You see, I am married to a preacher. My husband is one of those zealous preachers who hits the pulpit and shouts when he proclaims God's Word. My favorite preachers have always been the type of preacher my husband is. Jack uses the same methods the preachers in the Bible used, and I admire their zeal and courage in proclaiming God's Word.

However, I learned early as a preacher's wife that it is quite different to read about the zeal of the prophets of old than it is to see the zeal of your husband as he displays it in front of God and everyone. How easy it would be for me to become his critic and to hurl sarcasm his way after one of his sermons. After all, preachers often say that their wives are their best critics. I am sure David would have said that about Michal also. But look what happened to her!

2. **A wife should *not* be critical of her husband or of God's man**. No place in the Bible does it teach us that God appoints a wife to critique her husband's spiritual life. Nor does it teach us that God places certain women in a church to analyze the pastor's sermons and his other dealings in the church. We do have Michal's story in the Bible to warn us of what happens to a woman who appoints herself chief judge of her husband or pastor.

3. **Punishment is meted out to a woman who appoints herself to criticize her husband or God's man**. The Bible says that Michal had no children until the day of her death. I do

not think God has to punish a woman who is critical and sarcastic with her husband. There is a **built-in** punishment for a woman who does this because sarcasm causes a woman to lose the romantic interest of her husband. I wonder whether **God** really directly punished Michal in this instance or whether she punished herself by making herself undesirable to her husband — so undesirable that he did not come in unto her in a romantic way for the rest of their marriage? Michal definitely suffered the consequences of her sarcasm more than her husband did.

4. **If a wife does not wish to become critical of her husband, she must guard her thoughts toward him**. Michal first despised David in her heart, then she spoke those feelings toward David through her sarcasm. When a woman thinks negatively about her husband, it is too easy to slip and say something she shouldn't say to her mate. If she wants to avoid saying something she shouldn't and reaping the consequences, she must choose carefully the thoughts she thinks about her husband. A single negative thought such as, "Oh, I wish my husband had taken out the garbage this morning," if mulled over throughout the day, can turn into a feeling of resentment. That feeling in turn brings about hateful and cutting words destined to kill the romance of a marriage. **It is possible to feel hatred toward someone we once loved!** Michal's story is evidence of this fact. It is also sound proof that it is possible to despise someone even after you have saved his life!

5. **Caring too much about what others think causes a wife to think wrongly about her husband**. Michal was embarrassed about what the other women in Israel would think about her husband's behavior. I wonder how many preachers' wives sit in pews worrying about what others (especially the women) think about their husbands' messages rather than concentrating on what God thinks about their attitudes toward their husbands and God's men. Michal should have been looking out for David's best interest — as she did when she saved his life. She should not have been thinking about how David's behavior would affect her reputation with the other

women in the community.

6. **Comparing her husband with other men causes a
wife to think wrongly toward him**. In II Samuel 3, we find an
account of Michal leaving David for a while and becoming the
wife of another man. Perhaps it was this period of unfaithfulness
which caused Michal to criticize David. Perhaps she was
comparing David to her former husband.

7. **A wife becomes a critic and snare to her husband
when she does not share his love for Christ**. David was
leaping and shouting for joy before the people because of his
excitement about the ark of the covenant being returned to
Israel. He was praising God because His Spirit was once again
returned to David's kingdom. David was called a man after
God's own heart, and it is obvious in this story that he wanted
nothing more than to know and to display God's power before
God's people. The love for God which David felt in his heart
was certainly on display at this time.

It is a shame that Michal didn't feel the same way about the
power of God. It is unfortunate that she didn't feel the same
praise and love for God that David did. Perhaps if she had, she
would have run down to the street and joined David in his
rejoicing rather than just peeking at him through a window. How
sad that when Michal did come out to greet David, she greeted
him with sarcasm rather than with sincere love and praise.

As a preacher's wife, I have seen and heard my husband
preach to heights of ecstasy about his praise and love for God.
I have felt and seen the Spirit of God work, and I must confess
that I have not in every instance been able to completely
understand the workings of the Spirit in my husband's life. Nor
have I been able to keep up with him spiritually well enough to
share in all of his rejoicing. Yet I have striven to respect and
reverence my husband as the Bible teaches me that I should,
and I have learned not to voice my questions about things which
I do not understand.

As I have given my best not only to share Jack's ministry,

but also to give more love and praise to the One Whom my husband loves, I have come to better recognize and appreciate the Spirit of God as He works in my husband's ministry rather than critiquing Jack's service for Christ.   This attitude has brought about a spiritual intimacy which enhances every other aspect of our marriage.

I pray that the Spirit of God, so important and needed in our lives and ministries, will never depart from us.

Bathsheba —
A Lesson on the Price of Sin

*"For the wages of sin is death;
but the gift of God is eternal life
through Jesus Christ our Lord."*
(Romans 6:23)

Chapter 19
Bathsheba
11 Samuel 11, 12

*D*AVID WAS NOT WHERE he was supposed to be; at the time when kings go forth to battle, David tarried at Jerusalem. While he tarried there, he saw from the rooftop of the palace a very beautiful woman bathing herself. David enquired who this woman was and found out she was the wife of Uriah the Hittite. The Bible says that David *"sent messengers, and took her."* (II Samuel 11:4a) I am not sure whether she went willingly or not. However, Bathsheba became pregnant and somehow delivered the message to David that she was with child.

David probably knew how this would make him look in the eyes of the people; so he called for Bathsheba's husband, Uriah, to return from battle. David tried to make it look like he had called Uriah just to enquire how the battle was going. Then David encouraged Uriah to go home and spend the night with his wife before he returned to fight. David also, probably feeling guilty, sent some meat with Uriah, perhaps so he could enjoy a special evening with Bathsheba. Maybe then Uriah would believe that it had actually been **him** that made Bathsheba pregnant and David's reputation could be saved.

Uriah, though, was some kind of dedicated soldier. He refused to go in unto his beautiful wife with whom he had not been for some time. He would not even sleep inside his own home. He just did not feel right enjoying the companionship of his wife when his fellow soldiers were fighting on the battlefield. I admire that kind of dedication!

That dedication, however, didn't solve David's predicament. So David called Uriah to him again and, of all things, David got Uriah drunk in hopes that Uriah would then go home to his wife. Though Uriah did get drunk, he still did not go to Bathsheba.

As the plot continues, I am reminded of the old saying, "Oh, the tangled web we weave, when first we practice to deceive." David, whom God called "a man after his own heart" plotted to have Uriah murdered. He asked Joab to place Uriah on the front lines of the battle so that he would be killed there. Joab risked the entire army's safety by moving them too close to the enemy in order to put Uriah on the front lines, and Uriah was killed. Joab sent a messenger to David to report on the battle and the resulting death of Uriah the Hittite. The Bible says that Bathsheba went through a period of mourning for Uriah, *"and when the mourning was past, David sent and fetched her to his house, and she became his wife, and bare him a son."* (II Samuel 11:27a)

The prophet Nathan came to David and gave one of the greatest object lessons in the Bible. Nathan used a story about a shepherd and his pet sheep. David related with this story because David had at one time been a shepherd himself. Through his object lesson, David became angry at the offender Nathan described before he knew his name. In fact, David said to kill the man; and Nathan replied by saying, *"Thou art the man."* (II Samuel 12:7a)

Because of Nathan's wisdom in communication and, I believe, because of the tenderness of David's heart, David immediately repented. However, it was too late. David had already *"displeased the Lord."* (II Samuel 11:27b) There was a price on the sin which David and Bathsheba committed. The baby was born, and the baby died. As long as the baby was sick, David stayed in seclusion and mourning, probably praying and fasting that the baby would be spared. But when the baby died, David cleaned himself up and ate a meal. His mourning was over as he said, *"I shall go to him, but he shall not return to me."* (II Samuel 12:23c)

Yet David's life would never be the same. Much more heartache would come to David and Bathsheba because of this terrible sin. However, God is ever merciful and forgiving. As David was comforting Bathsheba, a child was conceived whose name would be Solomon. Bathsheba became the mother of a truly great king whose wisdom in Proverbs is a tribute to the wonderful things that his mother taught him. Yet even Solomon struggled later on in his life, perhaps because of the character weaknesses which he saw in his own mother and father.

This story, which is related in II Samuel 11 and 12, ends with a beautiful illustration of friendship. Joab had fought long and hard against the Ammonites and had conquered the royal city. Joab knew that he was about to win the war. He knew that if he did win the war without King David being present that the people would anoint Joab as king. Joab was extremely loyal to King David, the person whom God had anointed to be the king. He knew better than anyone the weaknesses of King David, but he was loyal to him anyway. So Joab called for David and encouraged him to come on over and help finish the battle. Joab wanted to make it look like David had won the war instead of him.

David did the gravy job and finished off the battle, so to speak, and Joab put the crown of the Ammonite king on the head of David and gave to David the glory which Joab rightfully deserved. What a friend! What loyalty!

Though this story is full of great Christian examples, Bathsheba is the lady of the story and hers is the life from which I drew the following lessons:

1. **I learn from the life of Bathsheba how important it is for a woman to protect herself from being a temptation to other men or from allowing herself to be**

tempted. Bathsheba needed to be more cautious in avoiding temptation or being a temptation because she was beautiful. Each Christian lady should be careful to be modest about displaying what beauty the Lord has given her. Certain beauties about a woman should only be displayed to her husband.

Bathsheba needed to be more cautious in avoiding temptation because she had been separated from her soldier husband for a long time. As much as possible, I believe that a husband and wife should avoid long separations. To me, there is rarely a legitimate excuse for a wife to be away from her husband for weeks or even for days at a time. I'm sure wartime was a legitimate excuse, but Bathsheba should have been wary and cautious about the temptations which this would place upon her.

My husband travels and preaches some around the country, and I pray and plan in a special way during our separations so that we might remain faithful to each other and pure in our lives. We rarely stay away from each other or remain too independent of each other for very long. A Christian couple can avoid David and Bathsheba's mistake by planning special times together, especially after being apart. When a husband and a wife are separated for ministry reasons, a wife should be loyal to her husband's dedication to the Lord just as Bathsheba should have been loyal to her dedicated husband, Uriah.

2. **I learn from the life of Bathsheba the importance of being more loyal to Bible principles than to people or positions**. It is not clear to me whether Bathsheba participated willingly in what happened, but I suppose it is improbable that she did not consent at some point. Probably David's very title intimidated Bathsheba into thinking that she had no choice about what happened.

I believe strongly in being loyal to my loved ones. I believe in being loyal to family, to friends and to God's servants. However, I must have more loyalty to the Bible, and I cannot allow my loyalty to my loved ones to cause me to violate the principles of the Word of God. Every Christian lady, when counseling or working with a man other than her husband, should not allow the man to cause her to do anything which she feels would violate a Bible principle or place undue temptation upon herself or someone else. No matter what the position, no matter who the person, purity should be a priority in our lives.

3. **I learn from the life of Bathsheba that there is always a price on sin**. I'm sure Bathsheba must have struggled with guilt if not with sincere and deep sorrow when she mourned the death of Uriah. Yet after the period of mourning was past, she became the wife of the king. It seemed that things were working out pretty well after all. The joy would be bitter though. The precious baby that Bathsheba carried in her body for nine long months would suffer with a lingering illness and then die. Having two children myself, I realize how much a mother loves her child, even when that child is only a newborn. I know how hard it is to watch your child suffer. I can't imagine the pain of losing a child. Never again would David's family be completely whole. Tragedy after tragedy would take place among his loved ones and would remind David of his mistake.

4. **I learn from the life of Bathsheba that God does forgive and use again those who have "displeased" him**. How sweet that, as David comforted a mourning Bathsheba, God allowed a child to be conceived in her sorrow. That child would be Solomon, the great and wise king, who would write the book of Proverbs and who would refer to his mother's teachings. God did forgive Bathsheba, and He used her to become a great mother.

Though God does forgive, though God will use us and bless us after we have sinned greatly, still our sins will follow us for years to come. We see this in the life of Solomon. I can picture beautiful Bathsheba with Solomon on her knees teaching him the truths of God. I can hear her saying lovingly, *"What, my son? and what, the son of my womb? and what, the son of my vows? Give not thy strength unto women, nor thy ways to that which destroyeth kings."* (Proverbs 31:2, 3) What Bathsheba was saying was, "Don't make the same mistake your father and I made."

Yet Solomon did destroy himself, and he destroyed himself through his lust for women. Though God used him, Solomon eventually did follow in the footsteps of his parents. How much better it can be if we can say to our children, "Do what I did" instead of "Don't do what I did." May this be the way it is in our lives. I believe it can be if we learn from Bathsheba and remember the price on sin.

Two Harlots —
A Lesson on Unselfishness

❦

"Verily, verily, I say unto you,
Except a corn of wheat fall into the ground and die,
it abideth alone: but if it die,
it bringeth forth much fruit."
(John 12:24)

Chapter 20
Two Harlots
1 Kings 3:16-28

*T*WO HARLOTS CAME TO Solomon. The first one said that, during the night, the other harlot had overlaid her son and he had died. The first harlot claimed that the other had placed her dead son beside her and had taken the living child for herself. The other harlot denied this, saying that just the opposite had happened. There were no witnesses to prove who was telling the truth, but wise Solomon knew just what to do.

Solomon asked one of his servants to bring him a sword so he could cut the baby in half. The false mother said, "Divide him." The real mother's heart yearned for her son and she said, "No! Let him live! Give him to the other woman." By this, Solomon knew who was the real mother. He awarded the baby to his rightful mother, the one whose heart had yearned for her boy. In this little story are some wonderful lessons on motherhood.

1. **A mother who has genuine love for her children will be unselfish**. She will want what is best for her children even if it means personal sacrifice. We live in a generation which doesn't like to sacrifice. This story in I Kings doesn't sound so strange when we realize that unborn babies are being "cut in half" at the rate of at least a million a year in the United States because they are considered an "inconvenience." Christian women cringe in disgust at both the story in I Kings and at the

rising abortion rate, and rightly we should. After all, abortion is not really about free choice or about a mother's rights. It is about communism, humanism, atheism and a woman's right to be like a man.

It is hard to understand the extreme selfishness which exists in the hearts of women who abort their own children. Yet even women who detest abortion and its sinfulness take part all too often in the sin which lies at the root of abortion: selfishness.

I have a sister, Becky, who is stricken with the disease of lupus. She works full-time in spite of her illness, but she must rest most of the time that she is at home. Because of this, I have kept her children — Trina, Teresa and Trent — at the top of my prayer list through the years. I thought it would be hard for them to turn out right with a mother who was unable to be a mother so much of the time. My niece, Teresa, is now in her sophomore year at Hyles-Anderson College. Since my husband and I teach there, we have been able to get to know her much better these past few years. To be honest, it has surprised me what a poised and sweet Christian lady Teresa has become.

A few weeks ago, Teresa told me how important her mother had been in her life. She proclaimed her mother (my sister) to be the "greatest mother in the world." I wanted to know just how a mother goes about being the "greatest mother in the world" when she has lupus, so I asked Teresa about it. Teresa explained that her mother never complained about her illness, but that she would drop anything to care for one of her children when they were sick. Teresa said that her mother was a very giving and unselfish person. I was reminded in a new way that our methods of motherhood are not as important as our ability to teach the greatest lesson of all — the lesson of unselfishness.

Since Teresa spoke those words to me, I have striven in a new way to not complain though it seems that my junior-high-age daughter is forever needing me to take her somewhere and to give her some money for this or that. I wish to teach my daughter the genuineness of my love through unselfishness. Of course I fail, but I try; and, of course, it is the Holy Spirit of God Who can give me the power I need to truly be an unselfish mother.

2. **A selfish mother doesn't care when others are hurt as long as she can have her pride satisfied**. The false mother didn't care if another life had to be taken. If she could not have her baby, she didn't want the real mother to have her baby either. It is especially difficult to be unselfish in times of grief and loss. For example, it is hard for the widow to be happy for those who are happily married. During times of grief and loss, it is especially important that we fight selfishness in our own lives.

3. **Selfishness is the root of many sins**. The false mother's selfishness led to lying. She lied to her friend and to King Solomon. Selfishness leads to stealing. The false mother stole a precious life from its mother. Selfishness leads to murder. We see this in the life of the false mother in the Bible. We also see it in the lives of the mothers who abort their babies daily in this nation. Though Christian mothers should hate abortion, we should also learn to hate the selfishness which we see in our own lives. This is one of the root causes of abortion.

As I am writing this chapter on unselfishness and remembering the selfishness of our country and its mothers, I am reminded of the words of Isaiah 49:15: *"Can a woman forget her sucking child, that she should not have compassion on the son of her womb? yea, they may forget, yet will I not forget thee."*

It's sweet to know that our omniscient God knew about the abortion rate of 1994 when He inspired this verse. There is nothing so unselfish as the love of a nursing mother. Yet even mothers can be selfish. They can be selfish enough to murder their own babies. God knew that and reminded those children that He would never forget them. When I fail my own children through my own selfishness, God will always be there for them, remembering them and loving them unselfishly. Yet I want to be there for them also. I want to be the mother that God would be if He were here. And so I pray that I would be there for my children today, driving the "taxi," giving the needed dollars for this or that activity, doing the repetitive tasks of motherhood, and mostly, loving unselfishly all the while with the love of a mother that can come only from God.

The Queen of Sheba —
A Lesson on Being Genuine

❧

*"Howbeit I believed not the words, until I came,
and mine eyes had seen it: and, behold,
the half was not told me."*
(I Kings 10:7a)

Chapter 21
The Queen of Sheba
1 Kings 10:1-13

*T*HE QUEEN OF SHEBA had heard of the fame of Solomon. She heard his testimony and knew of his relationship with the Lord. She came to visit Solomon for the purpose of proving his authenticity and his genuineness by asking him difficult questions. She communed or poured out her heart to Solomon in intimate conversation. It seems that she was diligently and yet skeptically seeking something, probably some evidence of the true and living God. The queen brought gifts with her, probably as a means of trying to purchase what she was so desperately seeking. Solomon took time with this queen and answered all of her questions.

The Bible tells us that the Queen of Sheba was extremely impressed by what she saw when she visited Solomon. She said that what she saw was at least double what she had heard about Solomon's greatness. The queen expressed that she was impressed by (1) Solomon's wisdom, (2) Solomon's house, (3) Solomon's food, (4) the clothing of Solomon's servants, (5) the happiness of Solomon's servants and, (6) Solomon's faithfulness to church.

After the Queen of Sheba investigated these areas of Solomon's life more closely, the Bible says that there was no more spirit in her. Her sarcasm and her questioning were gone. She did not believe what she had heard about Solomon until she saw it. It seemed too good to be true. But when she saw it, she exclaimed, *"The half was not told me . . . ."* She responded by glorifying Solomon's Lord and by exchanging gifts with Solomon before her departure.

When the Queen of Sheba visited in the home of Solomon, she found him to be genuine. I often wonder what people's response would be to me and to the average Christian wife and mother if they investigated our homes and the things which the Queen of Sheba investigated.

I speak and teach as well as write often on what a Christian lady should be, particularly as a wife and mother. Those who hear my teachings and read my writings know me from a distance. It has always been my desire that if those listeners and readers should visit in my home and investigate my life more closely, they would find my Christian walk and my love for my family to be truly genuine. As a preacher's daughter and a preacher's wife, I am aware that I am often being watched and examined in my Christian life. I realize that my marriage is examined as well as other things. I used to almost rebel at that responsibility and the pressure which accompanies it. Now I realize how fortunate I am to have the opportunity to represent Christ as Solomon did.

I also want the parts of my life which are not closely examined by others to be found to be genuine and authentic. It is the areas of our lives which no one will ever see which truly depict the authenticity of our Christian walk. Because I am a full-time housewife and only work part-time at my other endeavors, I am alone a lot of the time. I make it a goal when I am alone not to do anything, watch anything on television, listen to anything, read anything, or say anything which would prove my Christian walk to be hypocritical. I also try to put into practice in my marriage and family life the things about which I teach and write. I am not completely consistent in these areas, but I do not teach or write about anything which I do not sincerely try to make an integral part of my own home. After all, I never know when someone may drop by for a visit. Of course, God sees everything we do, and He is the One we should truly strive to be pleasing.

When people occasionally have reason to step into my home and into the part of my life that most people do not see, I have a rare chance to show them the genuineness of my life in Christ and of His love in my home. The story of the Queen of Sheba in I Kings 10 shows us what a powerful impact such times can have on our testimony and in the lives of others.

Let me mention again the things the Queen of Sheba saw in Solomon's personal life which took away her questioning spirit and replaced it with a conviction that what she had heard about Solomon and His God was indeed the truth. These are things that we as Christian wives can copy, thereby demonstrating our authenticity.

1. **Solomon's house**. Of course, my home cannot compare to Solomon's house in its grandeur. It cannot even come close. But should it be investigated by an outsider, I pray that they would find it clean and neat. I pray that they would find it free of magazines, videos, books, etc. which would be dishonoring to the Lord.

2. **Solomon's food**. The Queen was astounded by the meat on Solomon's table. My grocery supply and dinner menus could not in any way compete with the gourmet delicacies which most likely graced Solomon's table. Yet I pray several times a week that God would help me to buy the right groceries for my family. I pray that I would cook as I should to care for the four "temples" of the Holy Spirit who live at my house.

Sure, I have to clip coupons and watch for sales. At times, the roast gets put back in the grocery store freezer; hamburger is placed in the cart instead. Yet should you eat a meal with us, I hope you would find a welcoming table, a nourishing meal and a peaceful atmosphere; most of all, I hope these things would help you to understand the greatness of our God Who has provided it all.

3. **The clothing of Solomon's servants**. My family and

I do not always dress in the finest of fabrics or in clothes bought from the most expensive of stores. In fact, I most of the time prefer thrift stores to expensive boutiques. It helps me to relate with people I love, as well as to stretch the budget. But I pray you would always find my family dressed neatly and warmly. I pray that my husband's appearance would glorify him as well as my Lord. I pray that should you stop in unexpectedly, you would never find us dressed in anything immodest or sloppy which would seem to contradict our Christian testimony.

4. **Solomon's faithfulness to church**. My family and I love to go to church. Yet I am aware that we could skip from time to time without anyone really knowing why we're not there. To stay home without a good reason would be contrary to the public testimony which my husband and I have presented. We cannot be sincere unless we are consistent in this area of our lives.

I have neighbors who know whether or not we are in church **every** Sunday and Wednesday. Especially on occasions such as holidays or special televised sports events, I wish to be in my place in church. Why? Because if Solomon's consistency to church changed the life of the Queen of Sheba, it could change the hearts of my neighbors also.

5. **Solomon's wisdom**. I hope that if you spent some time just following me around, you would find me seeking the Lord's help in every decision. I hope you would find the ordinary things like scheduling a day of housework to have been thought out carefully and prayerfully as if all of my students and readers were watching. Someone much more important **is** watching! I hope you would find me seeking advice from the proper places — such as from my husband and my pastor — as I make even the seemingly insignificant decisions of life.

6. **The happiness of Solomon's servants**. I hope and pray more than any other thing that you would find in my home a truly joyful family relationship. I hope you would find it to be what my husband's preaching and my teaching portray it to be. I believe should you live with us for a while, you would find us

to be imperfect and very human. Yet I believe you would also find us to be truly sharing the love of Christ with one another.

I pray you would find my children to be joyful in knowing the love of Christ and the unselfish love of sincere parents. Nothing betrays a wife or a mother's testimony more than the sour attitudes of those who live with them or know them best. Nothing can exalt the Lord and the testimony of a wife and a mother more than the joyful spirits of her loved ones.

Again let me say that if you visited in my home you would definitely find inconsistency and failure from time to time. Yet I endeavor — and I challenge every Christian wife to endeavor — to be truly genuine in her Christian walk within the walls of her own home and with her own family.

Too many Christians who have advertised their Christian walk by way of televised programming have been found in recent years to be completely inconsistent in their private lives. We need a revival of wives and mothers who desire and strive to be their **sweetest** and their **most spiritual** when no one notices. We need wives and mothers who greet the folks at home with **more** charm and courtesy than they do the folks at church.

I am not against being a good public testimony. Our public testimony is extremely important. I am against being less concerned about what we do in private than what we do in public.

I am convinced of the genuineness of my own parents. It is that genuineness which turned me toward the Lord. The way they spent their money in our home, the way they cared for our house itself, the way my mother cooked, the way we were clothed and cared for were all consistent with my parents' public testimony. Their faithfulness to build our lives around the church and to seek the Lord's wisdom in their daily decisions were to me a testimony to the authenticity of their Christianity. They were not perfect, but I am convinced that both were always sincere.

I want to be the same. I want the words I speak and the life I live before thousands of people at my church and wherever I minister to be a glorious testimony of the glory of the true and living God. Yet I want my home and all its private corners to also glorify His name and to speak of a Christian life which is authentic, genuine.

Should you visit our home, you would find much weakness — especially on the part of the wife and mother who resides there. But I believe you would also find a message which says, "God is real and God is good . . . and the half has not been told you." May this message be spoken loudly and clearly in every corner of every Christian home and in every Christian's private life.

Jeroboam's Wife —
A Lesson on Pretending

❦

"For the LORD seeth not as man seeth;
for man looketh on the outward appearance,
but the LORD looketh on the heart."
(I Samuel 16:7b)

Chapter 22
Jeroboam's Wife
1 Kings 14:1-18

THE RULE OF JEROBOAM had a wonderful beginning. Then, because of King Rehoboam's greed, God divided Israel into two parts. Two tribes followed Rehoboam and ten tribes followed Jeroboam. However, Jeroboam did not handle authority very well; it spoiled him, as it does so many people.

Jeroboam became jealous and afraid of losing his kingdom. He became so afraid that he would no longer permit his people to go to Jerusalem every year to worship the Lord. Instead, Jeroboam built idols and made a place for his people to worship nearby. Jeroboam's kingdom became an idolatrous kingdom, and God punished him by causing Jeroboam's son, Abijah, to become very ill.

Jeroboam commanded his wife to masquerade as someone other than herself. He told her to go to the prophet Ahijah to ask whether or not their child would live. Ahijah was old and could not see well. Yet God told Ahijah who was coming to see him, and Ahijah recognized her by the sound of her feet when she first stepped up to his door.

Ahijah revealed to Jeroboam's wife that he knew who she was and that her son would indeed die. He proclaimed God's anger toward Jeroboam for his idolatry and said that he would be punished in many ways because of it. Ahijah's prophecy came to pass immediately. As soon as Jeroboam's wife entered the threshold of her own house, her child died.

We are reminded in this story of the foolishness of pretending before God.

1. **It is foolish to pretend in our spiritual lives**. We may sit in the front in church, sing our hymns loudly and pray or speak piously. If this is sincere, then it is always a good testimony to love the Lord on the outside and in public. But if what is happening on the inside and in private is not consistent with the outside, God knows it. He also has the ability to reveal it to others.

The idolatry which Jeroboam and his wife practiced caused her to masquerade before the man of God. When Jesus is not truly first in our lives, we will not be able to be ourselves before others, especially before the man of God. I believe it is best for Christian ladies to be as transparent as possible, to be unafraid to reveal our humanity. When we become too practiced at being something we are not, it tempts us toward hypocrisy. I am not saying we should "let it all hang out" so to speak. But we should not try to display perfection as a way of impressing people. People are much more helped when they see our ability to overcome sin in spite of our human frailties. Also, God gets more of the glory that way.

2. **It is foolish to pretend in our marriages**. I believe in being happily married in public. After all, if marriage is to be a picture of the relationship between Christ and the church, surely God intends for the happily married husband and wife to illustrate that relationship. But a Christian wife should be **most** loving to her husband when she is at home and no one else sees. The wife one is in private is the wife she really is.

3. **It is foolish to pretend with our children**. One reason a Christian lady should learn to be transparent is because children cannot tolerate inconsistency in this area. It is hard for a child to understand why a mother acts so differently around the people at church than she does around her family at home.

True, most children could afford to learn not to be so much themselves in public. However, it's possible that what we all really need to learn is this:

A. We need to learn to be as well-mannered at home as we are in public.

B. We need to learn to be as reachable and transparent in public as we are at home.

When God revealed the deception planned by Jeroboam's wife to Ahijah, she learned that you can't deceive God. God knows what we are like in our private lives, and He has a way of revealing it to others. As Christian wives and mothers, let us not be so foolish as to pretend that we are something we are not. Let's not pretend before God and others. Let us ask the Holy Spirit to make the real us worth knowing, and let us allow people to know the part of us that is most real.

Jezebel —
A Lesson on Pride

❧

"Pride goeth before destruction,
and an haughty spirit before a fall."
(Proverbs 16:18)

Chapter 23
Jezebel
1 Kings 19:1-3; 21:1-23

$\mathcal{T}$HE NAME *JEZEBEL* HAS a very negative connotation. I have heard some ladies called Jezebel in jest, and I have interpreted it to be a negative form of teasing or slandering. I have heard cars called Jezebel when they would not run. Never have I heard the name Jezebel mentioned in a positive way.

I consider Jezebel to be one of the most wicked women who ever lived. I don't think I would want to be compared or identified with her in any way, shape or form. However, when I study the life of Jezebel, I realize that the mistakes she made are not all that uncommon. It is with shame that I realize that at times I **have** been like Jezebel in some ways. To illustrate how, let me share with you some of the events of Jezebel's life.

There are basically only two incidents in the Bible where Jezebel is mentioned as a main character. One is found in I Kings 19. We find there an account of Jezebel seeking to kill one of God's choicest prophets, Elijah. The second account of Jezebel's life is recorded in I Kings 21. We have there the story of a man named Naboth who owned a vineyard which was located close to the palace of King Ahab, husband of Jezebel.

Ahab desired to have the vineyard of Naboth because it was close to the palace. He promised Naboth a better vineyard or money in exchange for his vineyard, but Naboth refused to sell it to Ahab because it was an inheritance from his fathers. Ahab's response to Naboth's refusal to sell was to go to bed and pout. He refused to eat because he was so angry.

Jezebel asked Ahab why his spirit was so sad, and Ahab said, "Naboth won't sell me his vineyard." How childish is the spirit of Ahab in this story! Jezebel said in so many words, "Aren't you the king of Israel? Eat and be merry. I'll get you Naboth's vineyard." Then Jezebel devised a despicable plot to get her husband what he wanted.

Jezebel wrote letters to the elders and nobles of the city in Ahab's name and sealed them with Ahab's seal. She asked these men to put Naboth in front of a crowd of people and have two wicked men bear false accusations against him. After the false accusations were made, Jezebel wanted these men to carry Naboth away and stone him to death. Jezebel was able to find some men to do exactly as she had asked; Naboth was stoned to death, leaving the vineyard available for Ahab to take as his own possession.

The story I just relayed is disgusting and unbelievable, something to which it is hard for the average Christian lady to relate. At least, it is very difficult for me to relate to it, and I hope it is for you also. However, when I consider Jezebel's life, I find that I have also been tempted to violate — and sometimes am **guilty** of violating — the same principles that Jezebel violated. Jezebel's life is not **just** a life which should bring disgust; it is also a life from which we should learn valuable principles which can be applied to our own lives. Allow me to share some of them with you:

1. **A wife's desire in the Christian life and in the ministry should never be a desire for power**. Jezebel was impressed with and trusted in her husband's power as king of Israel. She felt she had the right to do as she pleased because Ahab was the king. She enjoyed and abused the power which her husband possessed and was angered when any power was denied her husband.

I am afraid that too many Christians can relate to this. They serve the Lord because they want to achieve a certain level of power or position. They are angry when someone else gets the position they wanted or when the position they have achieved is not significant enough for them. Many Christian wives get angry when their husbands are overlooked for certain tasks or for the ministries which they hoped they would be asked to perform.

I often remind myself that power or position is not the important element in the Christian life. I must not seek power in my Christian service, not for myself or for my husband. God's blessing is upon those who **serve** Him with a humble heart. If my husband and I are given some power, we must use it humbly for the glory of the Lord; we must not abuse it.

2. **A wife must not make her own plans to get her husband what he wants**. A wife should not seek for her husband a position which the Lord has not given to him. Rather, she should trust the Lord in this area. It sounds noble to some wives to seek out things for their husbands, especially position. However, we must realize that this is exactly the principle which Jezebel violated. She listened to the words of her pouting husband and then set out to get him what he wanted.

When a husband is disappointed about the things he wants and cannot have, a wife should handle his disappointment with the spirit of Christ. She should be an encouragement to him, but she should not handle his disappointment by attacking another Christian or by seeking the power which was denied her husband.

3. **A wife must allow her husband to be truly in charge**. Jezebel tried to make it look like Ahab was running his own show by using the king's name and the king's seal, but it was Jezebel who had taken matters into her hands and was running the palace. I do not wish to take over my husband's authority, even if it means getting him something he wants. When my husband suffers disappointment or discouragement, I still must encourage him to stand on his own two feet as the leader of our home. The key word here is *encourage*. This is my job as the follower in our home. My only other responsibility in

handling my husband's discouragement is to take the matter to the Lord and to trust Him and my husband with the results.

4. **A wife must remember that desire for power and lack of submission leads to evil**. Jezebel did one of the most evil things that a human being can do. She falsely accused Naboth as well as seeking to hurt and kill one of God's men, Elijah. A woman who does not resist the desire for power in her own life and in her husband's life, a woman who does not truly **follow** her husband in their home, will be more vulnerable and will be tempted to work evil toward God's servants.

The devil often uses wicked people to bring false accusation against others. It is frequently because of jealousy that comes when wicked people want something which someone else has. Jezebel's jealousy for Ahab eventually led to Naboth's murder. Destruction of others is the consequence of those who selfishly seek power for themselves or for their mates.

5. **A wife who desires power and lacks submission has an evil influence upon her family**. The Bible tells us in I Kings 21:25 that Jezebel stirred up the wickedness in her husband, Ahab. This is a tremendous picture of the influence that a wife has upon her husband. A wicked wife will have a wicked husband. A wife who seeks power and is not right with authority will have a husband who seeks power and is not right with authority.

Elijah rebuked Ahab and Jezebel after the murder of Naboth. When Elijah did so, Ahab repented in sackcloth. The Bible says nothing about the repentance of Jezebel. However, because of Ahab's repentance, God decided not to punish him. He decided instead to punish Ahab's sons. Jezebel's sons had to bear the punishment for the wrongdoing which Jezebel commandeered.

Jezebel also had a daughter named Athaliah. Athaliah's desire for power was even greater than her mother's desire. This desire for power was the driving force which caused her to commit even more grievous evil than her mother did.

Athaliah's husband became king. When he did, Athaliah had all of her brothers-in-law killed so that they could not overthrow her husband's kingdom. When Athaliah's husband died, her son, Ahaziah, took his place. Ahaziah had the priests of the Lord murdered — probably because of his mother's counsel. The Bible says that Athaliah was her son's *"counsellor to do wickedly."* (II Chronicles 22:3b) Ahaziah died of an incurable disease, and Athaliah seized the throne by attempting to have all her other blood relations killed. These relatives were her own grandchildren! One infant was rescued and protected by Athaliah's stepdaughter, Jehosheba. This infant child named Joash was proclaimed king when he was eight years old. Athaliah cried, "Treason!" and was killed at the palace gate. The Bible tells us that horses trampled her body and that no family or friends mourned her death.

We can see in this story the evil influence that Jezebel had on her daughter, Athaliah. *"As is the mother, so is her daughter."* (Ezekiel 16:44b)

6. **Those who commit evil against others, especially against God's men, are headed for an untimely and tragic death**. Jezebel reaped what she had sown and was thrown from a palace window by some of her enemies. Her blood splattered upon the palace walls and horses trampled upon her body. Her daughter, Athaliah, died in much the same fashion.

How tragic and despicable is the life of Jezebel! The Bible tells us that she was involved in a cult which worshiped false gods. The prophets of these false gods were fed at her own dinner table. The deeds committed by this woman are almost unthinkable to Christian ladies like myself. Yet the principles violated and the motives behind these violations are not so unthinkable. Because of this, I choose to avoid these motives with God's help; I choose to live by a different set of principles. I choose to serve the Lord and others in a spirit of humility rather than with a desire for power. I choose to follow my husband through success and through disappointment, walking always as the follower and not the leader. I pray the Lord will make it so!

The Preacher's Widow —
A Lesson on God's Provision

*"But my God shall supply all your need
according to his riches in glory by Christ Jesus."*
(Philippians 4:19)

Chapter 24
The Preacher's Widow
11 Kings 4:1-7

*T*HE STORY IN II KINGS 4:1-7 is the story of a woman who was both the granddaughter of a preacher and the wife of a preacher. Her husband had been a servant to Elisha. Her husband had died, however, and this widow woman had a debt she could not pay. A creditor had come to take away her two sons in payment of the debt. He would use them as slaves.

The widow woman wisely ran to the man of God for help in her time of need. She ran to Elisha and reminded him of the fear that her husband had had for the Lord. Elisha was ready to help — as every Christian should be in another's time of need. He asked the woman, *"What shall I do for thee? tell me, what hast thou in the house?"* (II Kings 4:2a)

All the woman had in her house was one pot of oil. Elisha commanded the woman to borrow from her neighbors **all** the vessels she could find. He then advised her to go into her house, shut the door and start pouring until every vessel was full. The widow woman wisely followed the advice of the preacher. She poured and poured and poured until she came to the last vessel she had been able to find. The Bible says that as soon as there was not a vessel more, the oil stayed. In other words, she could not have poured it out on the floor. When the vessels were filled, the oil was gone.

The woman told Elisha what had happened, and he told her to sell the oil and to pay her debt. There are many sweet lessons about the provision of God that the Christian wife can learn from this story.

1. **God provides for the family of the preacher**. It is sweet to me how many times in the Bible God provided for the family of His servants. This is especially sweet to me as I am the daughter of a preacher, the wife of a preacher, and the mother of a preacher's granddaughter. It is sweet to see how God blesses a godly heritage.

2. **God provides for the wife of the preacher**. A preacher and his wife have few earthly possessions to claim as their reward for their labors. The fruit of their labors is in the lives they have won and influenced. Often a preacher cannot afford much in the way of expensive life insurance.

When we are tempted to become greedy and to lose sight of the real focus of our husband's ministry, when we are tempted to fret about the future, let us as preacher's wives remember that God has his own life insurance plan for the wife and family of the preacher.

3. **God provides for the woman whose husband fears the Lord**. When the widow went to present her problem to Elisha, she reminded Elisha that her husband had feared the Lord. I believe that God blessed this widow not only because her husband feared the Lord, but also because his wife had influenced him and allowed him to serve the Lord and to put God before monetary gain in his life.

It is difficult for the preacher's wife as she realizes that she will never be wealthy. While she may have friends who are laymen's wives and she may watch their husbands receive promotions and raises in pay in the business world, she realizes that this is not part of God's plan for her life. Christian service is not about promotions; it is about servanthood.

Yet if a wife will accept this fact and then encourage her husband in spiritual things, God will provide for her in ways greater than she imagined. These may or may not be material things, but they will exceed what her own plans could have obtained.

4. **Before God sends His blessing and His provision, He asks us to follow Him**. The widow woman had to seek God's blessing in the right place. So if we expect God's provision and blessing on our lives, we must not seek it from anyone other than God and His servants. The widow woman wisely went to the man of God to receive the help she needed.

A. The widow woman had to prepare for God's blessing in the right way. She had to heed the advice of Elisha or the blessing would not have come. We as wives must seek God's provision and blessing not through scheming, but listening to the Word of God as preached from the pulpit by God's man. We must obey the Word of God which we hear. It is then that we become what we should be, prepared to receive the blessings which God has for us.

B. The woman had to expect God's blessing with the right attitude. Elisha asked the woman to do something which seemed impossible. He asked her to pour one pot of oil into many vessels. He seemed to be asking her to make something out of nothing. If the woman was to receive God's blessing, she had to have enough faith to go ahead and do what might have seemed senseless. She had to expect that God had given her the right advice and that He was going to meet her needs.

5. **God will provide for the godly wife not only for today but also for her entire future**. Elisha told the widow to sell her oil, to pay her debt and then to live off the rest of the money. Not only was there money enough to pay the debt, but there was also enough for the widow to care for herself and for her two children in the future.

I do not believe it is wrong for a Christian worker to have life insurance or to have money put away for the future. Yet a Christian worker cannot have material gain as his focus and still accomplish what he should for the Lord. Time and time again, my husband and I gently remind each other that we must be cautious about seeking material gain.

Sometimes I still fret about the future and wonder if our needs will be met. It is wonderful to know that God does provide for the families of His servants and for the families of all of those wives who truly encourage their husbands to fear the Lord and to put Him first.

The Great Woman (The Shunammite Woman) – A Lesson on Hospitality

❦

"And whosoever will be chief among you,
let him be your servant."
(Matthew 20:27)

"And it fell on a day,
that Elisha passed to Shunem,
where was a great woman."
(II Kings 4:8a)

Chapter 25
The Shunamite Woman
11 Kings 4:8 -37

I ENVY THE WOMAN of Shunem because God Himself calls her a great woman. (II Kings 4:8) This great woman saw Elisha passing through one day, and she constrained him to stay and to eat at her house. So great was the hospitality of this woman that Elisha made this a regular habit. Every time he passed by the city of Shunem, Elisha had a meal with this woman and her husband.

The Shunammite woman was a woman of great perception for she told her husband that she perceived that Elisha was a *"holy man of God."* (II Kings 4:9) She asked her husband to help her prepare a chamber where Elisha could rest when he was passing through. She carefully furnished Elisha's little room with a bed, a table, a stool and a candlestick.

Elisha was so grateful for her hospitality and her care for the man of God that he asked her on one of his visits what he could do for her in return. Elisha offered to speak for her before the king, perhaps to find some type of royal position for her or her husband or to set up some type of special treatment. The Shunammite woman turned down Elisha's offer because she was content to dwell in her own town with her old friends and kinfolk.

So unselfish was this woman in her service to Elisha and so

content was she that Elisha had a difficult time deciding what he could do for her. I love the fact that Elisha was so in tune with God that when he heard the woman's husband was old and that she was childless, Elisha immediately told his servant Gehazi to run and get the woman. Elisha was going to tell her that the same time next year she would have a child. He and God seemed to confer quite quickly about this. Great must have been their confidence in each other. Sure enough, a year later, the great woman gave birth to a son.

After the child had grown a little older, he went to be with his father in the field and was stricken with a headache. The father asked a lad to carry the boy to his mother. The Shunammite woman held her son in her lap until noon when he died. The mother laid her dead son on Elisha's bed and shut the door. She then asked her husband to send one of the young men and a donkey so that she could go to the man of God.

Her husband asked why she was going and she simply said, *"It shall be well."* (II Kings 4:23b) The Shunammite asked the servant boy to drive quickly to Mount Carmel. When Elisha saw her coming, he asked Gehazi to go to her and to see if anything was wrong. The Shunammite woman told him that, *"It is well."* (II Kings 4:26c) When she reached the man of God, she grabbed his feet and began to behave bitterly. She told Elisha that she had not begged for the child; he had been a gift from God at Elisha's request and now he was dead.

Elisha seemed to know at once that God would raise the child for this great woman. He was, however, busy himself so he sent his servant Gehazi with a staff to go and raise the boy from the dead. The Shunammite would have none of that! She wanted the man of God himself to go with her, so Elisha complied.

When Elisha got to the house, he went into the room where the boy lay and prayed for him twice. The third time he went into the room, Elisha lay upon the boy's dead body — mouth upon mouth, eyes upon eyes, and hands upon hands. The flesh of the child began to warm. Elisha left the room and paced. He then returned to the room and stretched himself upon the child again. The child sneezed seven times and opened his eyes. Elisha called Gehazi and had him go get the Shunammite woman. When she saw that her child had been raised from the dead, she bowed herself. She then took up her son and went out.

What a wonderful story illustrating the greatness of God and what He can do with a man of God who remains closely in touch with Him. Yet I find myself the most intrigued with the qualities I see in this woman. Allow me to share with you the traits that I believe caused God to call her a great woman.

1. **A great woman has perception**. She recognizes godliness and respects it. The Shunammite woman had enough spiritual perception to recognize that Elisha was a holy man of God — as she told her husband in II Kings 4:9.

2. **A great woman is dependable**. Elisha trusted this great woman enough to visit her on a regular basis in time of need. I would like to be just as dependable in order to meet the needs of the man of God and of my preacher husband. If I am to be great, I must be the same every day (not moody) so that I can do my husband good all the days of my life. (Proverbs 31:12)

3. **A great woman is content**. She does not desire position. This is one of the characteristics of the Shunammite woman which stands out most in my mind. She was so content in her life that Elisha had a hard time finding a way to repay her for her kindness. When Elisha asked her what he could do, she had no suggestions. When he offered to speak for her before the king, she said that wouldn't be necessary. A great woman is content to give favors without expecting anything in return.

I often tell the students in my Christian Wife class at Hyles-Anderson College that the first and best thing they can do to begin to prepare to be a good wife is to learn to be satisfied and content with their present circumstances. The great woman of Shunem was such a woman.

4. **A great woman sees her lifelong dreams come true**. The Shunammite was not looking for a dream to come true

through her service to Elisha. She had no favors to ask of him. Yet her kindness caused her to be rewarded with a long-awaited son.

5. **A great woman sometimes lacks faith**. It is encouraging to see not only the greatness of the Shunammite woman, but also to see her humanness. When she realized that the child had died, she became desperate. After all, she had not asked for this child. It had been a gift from God and Elisha. Now that gift had been taken away from her. She shared these things with Elisha as if she were a woman scorned.

6. **A great woman knows where to go when her faith is small**. When the Shunammite woman needed help, she didn't bother her husband with it. She simply told him that all was well. She didn't bother Elisha's servant with it. She also told him that all was well. She didn't carry her problems from person to person seeking sympathy. She went straight to the man of God, and there she poured out her heart.

7. **A great woman is hospitable**. I have saved this point for last because I believe this is the quality about the great woman which God blessed the most and it is the quality about which I wish to write in more detail.

The characteristic of hospitality is greatly lacking in the lives of the women of the 1990's. So many women work full-time and have careers that they have quit trying to make the home a haven for their husbands and for those who visit.

I have done much study on the subject of marriage, and I am convinced that a man has a God-given need to have a wife who shows him hospitality regardless of how many hours she spends in the work force. I have discovered that no matter how much money the average woman makes, she still wants to feel that she is supported by her husband financially. On the flip side of the coin, no matter how much financial help a man gets from his wife, he still wants to be supported by her domestically.

I am not saying that a man cannot help his wife around the house. I am not saying that a wife should not work outside the home. I am saying that a woman should set aside some time to provide an atmosphere of hospitality for her husband in order to meet one of his most basic needs. That woman should guard this time and keep it as an important part of her schedule.

I love how the Bible takes the time to tell us the different items which the great woman placed in Elisha's chambers. She provided a restful atmosphere for the man of God, and she did it with care. God blessed her for that, and God calls her a great woman.

I do believe that God especially blessed the woman of Shunem because she was hospitable to the man of God. God has special blessings and bestows a special amount of greatness upon the woman who is hospitable and thoughtful to the man of God.

I would love to be called a great woman by God. Yet if this is to happen, I must forget the goal of greatness and seek to meet the needs of others — my preacher husband and other men of God in particular. I must not do this with a goal in mind to receive special favors from them. Rather, I must do it with great contentment. God help me to serve my husband and God's men in such a way that God could say that, in Indiana as well as in Shunem, there was a great woman.

Naaman's Maid —
A Lesson on Influence

*"Death and life are in the power of the tongue:
and they that love it shall eat the fruit thereof."*
(Proverbs 18:21)

Chapter 26
Naaman's Maid
II Kings 5:1-14

Dedicated to Linda Stubblefield

NAAMAN WAS A VERY important man in Syria as captain of the king's army. II Kings 5:1 tells us that Naaman was a great and honorable man to his master. The Lord delivered Syria through Naaman. The Bible tells us that *"he was also a mighty man in valour, **but he was a leper** ."* (Emphasis mine.)

Naaman had a little maid who had been taken captive out of Israel. This maid's responsibility was to serve Naaman's wife. Though this little maid was just a young girl, she had compassion on her mistress's husband, and she proclaimed to her one day, *"Would God my lord were with the prophet that is in Samaria! for he would recover him of his leprosy."* (II Kings 5:3)

God used this young girl to do something very special! He used some words, perhaps even carelessly spoken words, to point Naaman to the man of God. It would be a good idea for all of us to point others not only to the Lord, but also to some man of God when they are experiencing trouble. It doesn't take someone really talented to do so. Yet God can do mighty things with those who point others to the man of God. He did something mighty through Naaman's little maid.

Naaman's little maid influenced Naaman to be cured of leprosy. Naaman probably became a Christian at this time also. At the least, the Bible says that Naaman was convinced through his healing that the God of Israel was the only God. The little maid may have been too young to have memorized the Romans Road to Heaven, but she influenced a great man spiritually.

Naaman went to the prophet Elisha seeking healing from his leprosy. He expected Elisha to pray over him or to pronounce him clean. Instead, Elisha told him to wash himself seven times in the dirty Jordan River.

Naaman was angered not only that Elisha did not pray over him, but also that he did not choose a cleaner river in which Naaman could bathe himself. After all, how does one become clean in a dirty river?

This is so like my relationship with the Lord sometimes. His ideas don't always seem as good as mine. God's commandments are never complicated; it's just that they are often hard to accept. God's plan of salvation is so easy — so easy that it is sometimes hard for humans to accept.

Again Naaman received some good influence which saved his life. His servants talked him into at least trying to obey the orders which Elisha gave him. When he did, Naaman's flesh became like unto the flesh of a little child. God healed Naaman completely! God did not turn his flesh into the flesh of a grisled old war captain. He made it baby-soft. When God heals, when God saves, He does it completely. Our record is as clean as it was at our birth, for we have been born again.

This beautiful picture of salvation could not have been included in the Bible if Naaman's maid had not influenced him by speaking the right words at the right time and by pointing someone in the right direction. I wonder if Naaman's little maid walked closely with the Lord and had asked Him to guide her mouth that day? God surely used her words in a wonderful way that day. She even got herself a place in the Bible.

When studying this story, I can't help but think of all the

people whose words have pointed me in the right direction.

I think of my pastor and my father, Dr. Jack Hyles, who was the most positive influence in my life during my adolescent years. He often spoke words of praise to his youngest and most mischievous child. Many times I asked myself, "Mirror, mirror on the wall, Is there anything good in me at all?" During my teen years, the answer that came back was the words of praise my dad had spoken. I therefore concluded that I must have been a pretty okay person. After all, my dad thought I was wonderful. At the time, I wasn't sure why he did, but I knew he did! He pointed me in the right direction with his words.

I think of my friend, Linda Stubblefield, who was the first person to encourage me to write a book on marriage. She even made suggestions as to how I could do it and offered her help. I acted surprised at the idea, but in my heart I knew that Linda was talking about a dream which I had carried most of my lifetime. God used Linda to say, "Now is the time." After that, everything fell into place; and it was obvious that God had been behind Linda's words. I think of all the times Linda praised the words which I put on paper. At that time, my husband knew I was writing a book, but knew little about it. My parents didn't know about the book, and neither did anyone else. I became discouraged about it from time to time, and Linda was the only one to encourage me. She did so often.

Linda has been a real help to my mother as well as myself, and she often mentions that she is an unlikely friend for us. She calls herself a "country girl," and I guess she is accurate in saying that she is about as different from my mother, Mrs. Beverly Hyles, as night is from day. But when it comes to pointing people in the right direction and influencing people to their potential, Linda is an expert. Not only does she point people in the right direction, but she uses the abilities she has to help people get where they ought to be going.

I think of a friend, Vicki Mitchell, who gave me a phone call one summer morning. She did not know that I had driven for five hours the night before with my husband and family from a conference. She did not know that I had prayed and cried all the way home while my exhausted preacher husband slept. She did not know that some hurtful things had been said about my father and other preachers at this conference. My husband responded by preaching hard and strong, but I could see the hurt in his eyes.

Mrs. Mitchell did not know that I prayed and asked the Lord to give me a sign that He wanted me to continue writing and teaching. I felt like "throwing in the towel." Vicki Mitchell just picked up the phone one morning and made a call to my house. She called to thank me for my articles in *Christian Womanhood* and to encourage me to keep writing. Her words were detailed and sincere, and I hung up knowing I had received an answer to my five-hour prayer of the night before. I had received a phone call from God. Unless Vicki reads this chapter, she still does not know what that phone call meant to me. Though I have thanked her several times, I have never relayed the circumstances to her. But I have no doubt that the Holy Spirit directed Vicki to point me in the right direction. The influence of her words will never be forgotten. I have wondered many times since then if I have ever failed to pick up the phone to call someone when the Holy Spirit was trying to direct me. It matters not if I feel shy about what to say. I want to make that call!

I think of the two evangelists, unknown to me, who spoke at my husband's church when he was a teenager. Both asked him this question: "Have you ever considered full-time Christian work?" Both times that question was asked, my husband's heart burned with conviction. Those questions started the process of my husband's surrender to preach. We have not seen either of those evangelists since then, but they have had a part in our lives and in our ministries ever since. Why? Because they chose words which pointed my husband in the right direction.

Every morning, every wife and mother should yield her life and her tongue to the Holy Spirit. She should ask the Holy Spirit to control everything in her life and to give her the victory over the devil. We have such a tremendous influence over our

husbands and children. So many are the words which we speak
daily to those with whom we live and whom we know the best.
It is of utmost importance that we use those words to point our
loved ones in the right direction. Each complaint or criticism
which we speak to family and others is not just a way for us to
get something off our chests. It is a tool which the devil can use
to sway our families in the wrong direction. Yet, the positive
words which can be spoken as we do such menial tasks as
housework (tasks like a little maid would do) can be used to
influence either for good or for bad.

"Oh Lord, how important is every word that I speak before
You and others. Make my words fewer and more carefully
chosen. So great is the time and influence which I have with my
family. Speak and live through me so that my influence might be
right. Thank you, Lord, for all those You have used to point me
in the right direction. May I do the same for those with whom I
meet today. Amen."

Jehosheba —
A Lesson on Protection

❦

*"And he was with her hid
in the house of the LORD six years."*
(II Kings 11:3a)

Chapter 27
Jehosheba
11 Kings 11:1-12

ATHALIAH WAS THE WICKED daughter of Ahab and Jezebel. Her husband was Jehoram, the son of Jehoshaphat. Jehoshaphat was a good king who made an unholy alliance to go to battle with Ahab. Because of this league, Jehoshaphat's son became acquainted with and consequently married Ahab's ungodly and wicked daughter. Alliances in any cause with unsaved people always lead to wickedness — if not in the present generation, then in the next one.

When Athaliah's son, Ahaziah, was killed, Athaliah began to desire the throne for herself. She was much like her mother, Jezebel, in her pride and in her desire for position. Jezebel usurped her authority over Ahab and left her rightful place as a woman much like Athaliah usurped her authority over the kingdom.

To be sure that she could occupy the throne herself, Athaliah attempted to destroy all of the royal seed. She even destroyed most of her own grandchildren. This is unthinkable! It is unless we consider the mothers of 1994 who encourage their daughters to abort their unborn babies so as to save embarrassment over an illegitimate birth. Both are unthinkable!

There was a lady in the kingdom who was to surprise Athaliah in a deadly sort of way through her courage and protection, and that lady's name was Jehosheba. Jehosheba was the daughter of King Jehoram. She stole one of Athaliah's grandchildren — a baby boy named Joash, and she hid him in the house of the Lord.

In the seventh year, Jehoiada the priest revealed to the captains and leaders in the kingdom that Joash was alive; then these men plotted together to anoint Joash king and to destroy wicked Athaliah.

Joash was anointed king in the temple and, when Athaliah heard the noise, she came running to discover what was happening. When Athaliah saw what was happening, she cried, *"Treason, Treason."* (II Kings 11:14b) At this time, Jehoiada the priest commanded those soldiers who were already at their appointed posts to take Athaliah out of the temple and then to kill her.

Because of Jehosheba and her protection and care of Joash, a revival began in the land under the direction of seven-year-old King Joash and his mentor, the priest Jehoiada. How did Jehosheba become responsible for revival in the land? By protecting and nursing one little baby. This story gives many lessons on the dignity of motherhood.

1. **There is great potential in the work of motherhood or in the work of caring for one little child**. Our society today tries to de-emphasize the value of motherhood. This attitude has affected even our Christian circles. It is sometimes embarrassing for a mother to admit that she just stays home and cares for her children. But God can do great things through the life of one little child who has been cared for and trained properly. This is also an important lesson for every church nursery worker, baby-sitter, etc.

2. **A mother has an important role of protecting her child**. God used Jehosheba because she had the courage to protect one little child from that which was dangerous to him. A mother must also protect her child from the world and its dangerous influences. Not only must a mother be conscientious

enough to protect her child from physical danger, but she must also protect him from spiritual danger. I pray daily that the Lord would put a hedge of protection around my children and to keep them safe spiritually as well as physically.

It takes courage sometimes to say "no" to television, public schools, movie theaters, wrong music, etc. that would harm our children. But when we do this, we must realize that we are not only fulfilling a role of motherhood; we are also doing something great.

3. **The best place a mother can protect her child is in the church**. Jehosheba took baby Joash and his nurse to the temple and hid him there. When my children were about two weeks old, they went to church for the first time. They rarely have missed since then. Why? Because the church is an important place to protect children from the world. Our children receive their education from a Christian school which is a ministry of our local church. Why? Because the church is an important place to protect children from the world. When we do not protect our children in church, unholy alliances will form — like the marriage between Jehoram and Athaliah.

Joash was an orphan and did not have a home. Therefore, church was of even more importance to him. In most situations, the church is to complement (on a consistent basis) that protection which is provided for children in their Christian homes. In some cases, however, there is no Christian home. Therefore, the church is of even greater importance. We must remember not to complain when dirty bus kids soil the carpets of our churches. We must remember that they need our church to protect them. We can serve the Lord by yielding our protection to others' children as well as to our own.

4. **Not only should a mother protect her child, she should stay with her child**. I am not saying that a mother should never work and leave her children full-time with a baby-sitter. I think many times though, if not most of the time, it is unwise. Why? Because children don't need just our protection; they also need our time.

5. **Mothers who dignify the office of motherhood and offer their children time and protection can save America.** That is exactly what happened in this story, is it not? One woman gave protection, care and six years of her life to one baby boy by keeping him in church, and a nation was saved. Revival was begun. I wonder what one woman could do who would devote her time to protecting one little child. I wonder what one woman could do who would protect one little child by her faithfulness to church and to her time with her child. Oh, that America had a generation of mothers who cared enough to protect their children!

Esther —
A Lesson on Destiny

*"And who knoweth whether thou art come
to the kingdom for such a time as this?"*
(Esther 4:14b)

Chapter 28
Esther
Esther 1 - 10

*T*HE STORY OF ESTHER is perhaps one of the most appealing stories to females. My niece, Tami, says it is her favorite story in the Bible, and I'm sure that many females would agree with her. It is intriguing to think what it must have been like to have lived in the palace for twelve months preparing for a beauty contest. How interesting it is to think what it must have been like to have been Esther — to have been an orphaned Jewish girl who suddenly became a queen.

Let me say, however, that I do not believe it is **ever** right for a young lady to marry a heathen man like Ahasuerus. I do not know whether or not Esther was forced to marry the king. (Esther was a slave in captivity at the time.) If Esther chose to marry the king, she made a sinful choice. Yet, I admire Esther's character and the way God used her. Many lessons can be learned from Esther. Allow me to share them with you.

1. **Esther did not put priority on material things**. When the time came in the beauty contest for queen Esther to "walk down the runway" so to speak, she — like all of the other contestants — was offered *"whatsoever she desired"* to go before King Ahasuerus. (Esther 2:13) I'm afraid after spending twelve months in the king's palace, I would have developed some bit of snobbery. If I had been offered anything I desired from my

ladies-in-waiting at the king's palace, I fear I would have asked for a little bit of extra jewelry or perhaps a little bit of extra makeup. I would have been tempted to ask for many little extras to increase my chances of being chosen queen.

However, Esther 2:15 tells us that when Esther's turn came, *"she required nothing"* but what was appointed for her. Esther did not depend on material possessions to enhance her beauty or to increase her confidence in her ability to obtain success.

I am not saying that it would have been sinful for Esther to have asked for something extra. It is not any more a sin for a lady to wear makeup or jewelry than it is for a lady to wear clothes. Yet there is a definite difference between a lady who uses makeup and chooses her attire in order to make herself look her best for her husband and the lady who leans upon her physical glamour as a way to attract attention or to increase her self-esteem. This type of lady is easy to spot. Her makeup is overdone. She is excessively trendy in her wardrobe. She changes like a chameleon and tries every fad because she is trying desperately to feel good about herself through her appearance.

I have learned that my self-esteem and satisfaction should come only from Christ. As a female, I have been tempted to find esteem in "things," but I have found that there is no satisfaction in anything other than Christ. We can see in the lives of the popular actresses of our day what happens to the female who is leaning on her physical appearance for her identity. In the 90's, Madonna is a vivid example of this type of person. Every time she is photographed, her hair is a completely different color. Her clothing is increasingly outrageous and unappealing. Why? Because when we lean upon our beauty for our identity with others and self, we actually destroy our beauty. Not only do we mar our outward appearance, but we also lose the inner radiance which truly makes a woman beautiful.

2. **Esther's righteous spirit enhanced her physical beauty**. The same verse which tells us that Esther required nothing also tells us that Esther obtained favor in the sight of **all**

them that looked upon her. Esther 2:17a says, *"And the king loved Esther above **all** the women, and she obtained grace and favour in his sight."* (Emphasis mine.) I have no doubt that Esther possessed physical beauty. Yet I'm sure that **many** women took advantage of the opportunity to compete for queen. There must have been scores of them which possessed physical beauty. However, there must have been something about Esther which made her beauty more noticeable than the other women's. I know what that something was: it was her inner spirit. Anyone can use Maybelline, but few women possess a beautiful inner spirit. It takes years of character and discipline to develop a beautiful spirit. Many women rely so completely on their physical appearance that they never develop such a beautiful inner spirit.

At the beginning of each semester that I teach at Hyles-Anderson College, I am always overwhelmed by the beauty of the girls in my classroom. As I get older, I find that their beauty impresses me even more. Yet, a strange thing occurs at the end of each semester. I often find that the girls who seemed the most beautiful at first are not as attractive by the end of the semester, and some who seemed rather unattractive have suddenly become beautiful in my eyes. Why? Because I have had several months to discover the character of these ladies. I learn their punctuality, their alertness, and their diligence to study and work hard. These characteristics actually take away or add beauty to each of their lives. I wish that more females developed these traits in their own lives. My desire is to possess an inner spirit of character like Esther did.

3. **Esther possessed a feminine spirit which was revealed by her obedience**. The Bible tells us in Esther 2:20b that *"Esther did the commandment of Mordecai, like as when she was brought up with him."* Throughout the book of Esther, you will find that Esther followed the plans which her guardian, Mordecai, made for her — even to the point of risking her life.

I know that Esther was feminine **because** she was obedient. I have observed the women's libbers of my generation enough to know that lack of obedience produces a hard, masculine woman. A woman who is in her properly submissive role will grow more soft and feminine as she ages.

Let's face it! There is no way that a woman can prevent the loss of physical beauty which naturally comes with age. My grandmother, Mrs. Coystal Hyles, died at age 97; and I am afraid there was not much, if any, physical beauty left on her face at the time of her death. **Yet, she was feminine!** This example alone causes me to desire to be obedient and feminine in my spirit. While physical beauty fades with time, the inward characteristics — such as femininity or hardness — increase. I wish to be feminine because all that will be visibly beautiful when I am older is my inward feminine charm.

4. **Esther was destined**. Esther's cousin and guardian, Mordecai, took a stand for the Lord by refusing to bow before the king's assistant, Haman. This so angered Haman that he convinced King Ahasuerus to make a decree that all the Jews of the land would be killed on a certain day. Of course, Ahasuerus had no idea that his own queen was a Jew. Mordecai had told Esther to keep her nationality a secret, and Esther had obeyed.

When Mordecai heard about Haman's plan, he sought for Esther's assistance. Esther was extremely concerned about approaching the king to plead for the Jews, because it was against the king's law for the queen to enter into his presence without being summoned. The penalty could be death!

Mordecai insisted that Esther speak up for the Jews. Mordecai displayed great faith when he told Esther that he expected deliverance even if Esther would not cooperate. However, he encouraged Esther to be the Jews' deliverer by asking her this question: *"Who knoweth whether thou art come to the kingdom for such a time as this?"* Esther showed great faith by being willing to fulfill her destiny and by asking Mordecai to have the Jewish people pray and fast for her as she approached the king. Esther herself fasted and prayed; this showed her faith in the power of God.

I have something in common with Esther because I am also destined. In fact, I am destined three ways. First of all, my parents gave me to the Lord when I was born. Hence, I believe that I was born with a special destiny which I cannot shirk.

Secondly, I gave myself to the Lord when I was a young girl, causing the Lord to set me apart a second time for something special. I may have days when I wonder whether I was right in giving myself to the Lord for full-time Christian work, but that doesn't change the fact that the Lord has set me apart. Excuse my poor grammar, but I cannot "undestine" myself by deciding that I did not really mean it when I vowed to give myself to the Lord. It seems to me — from examples given in God's Word — that when God sets apart something (or someone), it is set apart for good.

Third, I am a preacher's daughter. In the Bible, the priestly tribe of Levi was allowed to marry only within its own tribe. That is that preacher boys were allowed to marry only preacher's daughters. This is "Schaapology" perhaps, but I believe that I was set apart by the very fact that I was born into a preacher's family. I am not saying that girls who are not preacher's daughters cannot make good preacher's wives. I **am** saying that preacher's daughters have a greater responsibility to the Lord. Add to this the fact that the firstborn child was set apart in the Bible days and — the most important fact of all — that God creates every human being to do something special for Him, and anyone reading this should be feeling pretty destined by now!

Not only are we destined, but we are destined *"for such a time as this."* I have discussed the woes of this world in the chapter on Lot's wife, but let me mention them again here. We live in a world which runs rampant with immorality and violence, even — and perhaps especially — among our children. We live in an atheistic, Satanistic society. This seems like it should be a reason for sorrow, but it is also a reason for hope. We can cry about the awful world in which we live, or we can commit ourselves to our destiny, to do for the Lord what is needed for such a time as this.

5. **Esther valued her destiny more than she valued her life**. When Mordecai asked Esther to risk her life in approaching the king, her answer was *"And so **will I** go in unto the king, which is not according to the law: **and if I perish, I perish** ."* (Esther 4:16c, emphasis mine.) It is no wonder that Esther was both beautiful and feminine. She was possessed with a destiny which caused her to forget about herself. I have never considered myself to be an extremely poised and feminine woman. When I have discussed this with my preacher father, he has always reminded me that femininity is not being self-conscious. Rather, it is losing yourself in the cause of other people.

I have always believed that the Bible teaches us in Genesis that the destiny of **every** Christian wife is to encourage her husband to do that which he is destined to do for God. No matter how great or small the task to which my husband is called, I believe I would rather die than to see him live and die having never done that thing which God made him to do.

The prayers and fasting of Esther and the Jewish people were looked upon with favor by God. The king favored Esther by holding out his golden scepter to her as a sign of his willingness to hear her request and to spare her life.

Esther showed the wisdom that comes from inner beauty and from seeking the Lord when she put on her royal apparel and prepared a banquet for the king and Haman. What man is not more ready to discuss problems on a full stomach! She honored the king even as she sought to undo one of his decrees. Her way of handling a problem between herself and her husband is in itself a great lesson to Christian wives.

Because Esther had already won much favor in the king's sight, he was enraged at Haman when he heard his plan and saw Haman treating his queen with disrespect. The story has a happy ending as we read that King Ahasuerus had Haman killed on the gallows that Haman had prepared for Mordecai. Haman's vacant position was filled by Mordecai. God showed His sense of justice by switching the places of Mordecai and Haman. The

Jews were spared and, best of all, Esther had fulfilled her
destiny. She had been in the place the Lord needed her, when
the Lord needed her. She had the inner character which
equipped her to fulfill the necessary task. She had the faith to
seek the Lord's help and to **do** what the Lord and His people
needed her to do. How sweet must have been her satisfaction!

How I pray that we as Christian women would also daily
put ourselves in the place where the Lord would have us to be.
I pray that, day by day, we will develop the inner character
which would equip us to do what the Lord needs to have done.
How sad for the Lord to find us too involved with the material
and the physical to have fulfilled His purpose for our days and
for our lives. How sad to live and die without fulfilling that
purpose for which we were created! How I pray that I do not
miss the destiny which the Lord has planned for my life!

Job's Wife —
A Lesson on Gratitude

❦

"Then said his wife unto him,
Dost thou still retain thine integrity?
curse God, and die."
(Job 2:9)

Chapter 29
Job's Wife
Job 2:9, 10

SHE WAS THE WIFE of an upright and very rich man. Job had provided her with ten children, seven sons and three daughters. They owned 7,000 sheep, 3,000 camels, 500 yoke of oxen and 500 female donkeys. The Bible says that they had *"a very great household."* (Job 1:3) The house itself must have been splendid as well as the possessions therein and the number of servants that were available to wait on them. Surely Job's wife enjoyed the days she spent sharing the wealth of her husband.

But tough times came upon Job. All ten of their children were killed. They lost all of their animals which represented the measure of their wealth. They lost most of their servants in death. In all this, Job's wife still had the most valuable thing I believe a wife can have. She had a spiritual leader who had not lost his integrity.

But things got worse. Job lost his health. He not only contracted a dreadful disease, he developed a disgraceful disease. To put it in modern terms, he contracted a gross disease. Still, Job did not lose his integrity nor did he lose his faith in God.

However, Job's wife became discouraged. I do not feel as harshly toward Job's wife as many people feel. I have not had to watch my husband suffer as Job's wife did. Yet I know from some limited experience that it hurts worse for a wife to watch her husband suffer than it does for her to suffer herself.

I do agree, however, that what Job's wife said and did in reaction to Job's troubles was wrong, very wrong. Job's wife found her husband sitting in an ash heap scraping himself, trying to relieve himself of the pain and irritation of a body covered with running sores. Job's wife, probably still mourning the loss of her children, seemingly began to mock Job by asking him a question. She said, *"Dost thou still retain thine integrity? curse God, and die."* Job rebuked her and reminded her of how good God had been to them. He felt it would be ungrateful to forsake God now in the midst of their troubles.

Though I feel some sympathy for the wife of Job, I am displeased with the way she treated her husband at a time when he needed her most. I feel that God must have been displeased also because He does not perpetuate her given name in the Bible. There are some lessons we can learn from this story which can help us to avoid the mistakes of Job's wife.

1. **It is ungrateful for a wife to share her husband's wealth and successes and then to desert him in times of trouble**. Job had provided very well for his wife. For many years, she had enjoyed more luxury than any woman in the east. Still, when Job lost it all, she was unable to remain loyal to him.

Many a wife has forsaken her husband and divorced him in times of trouble. I notice, however, that such a woman almost always wants her alimony checks even when she does not want to share her life with her husband any longer. Many an ex-wife will go to great lengths legally to be sure she gets some of her ex-husband's wealth. I am not against the principle of alimony, especially if a husband has forsaken his wife. I **am** opposed to a wife forsaking her husband and then insisting on being financially supported by him.

Whether a woman forsakes her husband or not, it is ungrateful for her to treat him differently when things are going poorly for him than she treated him when he was on top. It is also very contrary to the marriage vows.

2. **A wife must realize that the hard times in a marriage provide opportunities to prove her love and gratitude.** Job's wife had an opportunity to show her support not only for Job, but also for God. She had an opportunity, perhaps, to have her name in the Bible and to be a positive example for women for many generations. Instead, she is used as a negative example.

3. **A wife must pray that God will not allow her to be a temptation in her husband's life, especially when things are not going well.** Job's wife added to his temptation to quit. The devil used Job's wife in Job's life. God could have used her to be a great blessing, but she allowed the devil to use her instead.

4. **A wife must control her tongue when she and her husband are enduring troubles.** I don't know if there is a woman alive who has been through what Job's wife went through who would not have felt the words which she spoke. To lose one child in death would cause great grief, not to mention losing ten. To suffer yourself and then to watch your own husband suffer even more, losing his health and the respect of his peers, would place doubt in the heart of any woman. If only Job's wife could have bitten her tongue. If only she could have voiced her complaints to God rather than to Job. If only she could have trusted and walked with the Lord to the extent that she could have found the strength to speak positively and encouragingly or at least to say nothing at all.

We must learn from Job's wife that an important way to be loyal to our husbands in time of trouble is simply to keep our mouths shut. At times like this, we must not say anything unless it is encouraging. That kind of grace in trouble comes only from our walk with the Lord.

5. **A wife must realize that the greatest loss that can come to a Christian wife is for her husband to lose his spiritual integrity.** More than anything in all the world, I want

to have a husband who does in his life what God wants him to do. My goal is not to hinder him, but rather to encourage him in doing that. To me, to sacrifice God's will for my husband would be the greatest sacrifice. The thing I value most is the thing that Job's wife still had. She had a husband who maintained his spiritual integrity. If Job's wife had been truly grateful for what she **did** have, perhaps she could have mustered enough strength to have been an encouragement to Job rather than a discouragement.

6. **A wife must remember that God blesses commitment**. In spite of her cruel words to Job, his wife did stay with him through all his trials. God blessed her with ten more children — or maybe he challenged her with ten more pregnancies! Job's wife **was** faithful to her husband because she stayed with him. If only she could have kept her mouth shut during that time! If only she could have been grateful for what Job had provided for her in the past! If only she could have been grateful for what is God's greatest gift to a wife: a spiritual leader who retains his spiritual integrity when times are hard!

May every Christian wife be grateful for her spiritual leader and may she value his integrity. May every Christian wife be grateful for the provisions which her husband has shared. May we be grateful enough to be supportive and encouraging even when times are difficult. And in those rare times when we cannot find the strength to speak encouraging words, may we keep our mouths shut and force a smile which says, "I love you always, in the good times and in the bad."

The Right Kind of Daughter—
A Lesson on Honor

*"That our sons may be as plants
grown up in their youth;
that our daughters may be as corner stones,
polished after the similitude of a palace."*
(Psalm 144:12)

Chapter 30
The Right Kind of Daughter
Psalm 144:12

*T*HERE IS A SIMPLE phrase in Psalms 144:12 that has a lot of powerful teaching on how to be a good daughter. I have striven in my life to be what my parents would need in a daughter. Studying this verse has helped me a great deal in those efforts and has taught me wonderful lessons on being the right kind of daughter. This verse begins *"That our daughters may be as cornerstones."* I looked up the definition of the word *cornerstone* in the *Reader's Digest Great Encyclopedic Dictionary,* and the following are some lessons I gleaned from the definitions:

• **God intends for the right kind of daughter to be a source of strength which holds the family together**. A cornerstone is a stone uniting two walls at the corner of a building. The right kind of daughter will bring her parents closer together, not cause division between them. The right kind of daughter will bring her siblings closer to her parents and her parents closer to her siblings. She will bring her siblings closer to each other.

I am not saying that each family quarrel must be the responsibility and burden of the right kind of daughter. But a good daughter must strive to spread kind words spoken by family members about each other. She must do what she can to "put out the flames" when there is strife among family members. If every young girl were the right kind of daughter, there would be less quarreling among brothers and sisters. There would be more harmony in the home.

• **The right kind of daughter's life is inscribed with the teachings of her parents.** A cornerstone is often inscribed and is often made into a repository where historical documents are stored. I looked up the word *repository* and found it to mean *a place where secrets are hidden.*

The right kind of daughter is also a person in whom her parents can confide, knowing that their secrets will be safe with her. She will not criticize her parents by calling them the "old man" or the "old lady." She will not broadcast to her peers their mistakes or the things she does not like about them. She will publish good about them. She will overlook her differences with them. Their conversation is safe in her hands and in her heart.

• **The right kind of daughter gets her strength from the foundation of Bible reading and prayer.** A cornerstone is laid into a foundation. The right kind of daughter gets strength from digging a foundation deep in Someone Who is strong. She walks with and serves the Lord. He gives her the strength to be the right kind of daughter.

Psalm 144:12 also says she is *"Polished after the similitude of a palace."* The following are some lessons I learned from the definitions of the word *polish*:

• **The right kind of daughter is well-mannered in her appearance, in her speech, and in her behavior.** *Polish* means *refinement or elegance of style.* This is because she is aware that all of these things reflect the teachings of her mother and her father as well as of her Heavenly Father.

• **The right kind of daughter makes an effort *not* to be crude in her speech or in her behavior.** *Polish* also means *to be free from crudity, imperfection; to be complete.* The right kind of daughter realizes that this type of talk or behavior is a poor testimony of her parents. She does not attempt to be perfect, but she trusts her Lord to make her complete through the discipline which comes from her parents, knowing that the Lord chose her particular parents for her life.

- **The right kind of daughter "shines" in her love for her Lord and for her parents**. *Polish* means *to shine.* There are too many daughters, especially preacher's daughters like myself, who complain about the pressure they feel to live up to their parents' expectations. They sometimes rebel, even run away, in an attempt to flee this pressure.

In studying Psalms 144:12, it seems to me that maybe God intended us to feel some pressure to be a good example of Him and of our parents. I do not believe that God ever intended us to run away from pressure. There is pressure everywhere we go. God intended us to run to Him and to find in Him the strength to allow the pressure to refine us and to make us the example of our heritage He intended us to be.

The Bible says that Jesus is our Cornerstone. He is the Stone which holds the Christian family together. He is the One with Whom we can share all of our secrets. He is the Foundation of our Christian life. Praise the Lord for Jesus, our Cornerstone! Praise the Lord that we can be like Him when we strive to be the right kind of daughter!

The Strange Woman —
A Lesson on Purity

❦

"For the lips of a strange woman
drop as an honeycomb,
and her mouth is smoother than oil:
But her end is bitter as wormwood,
sharp as a twoedged sword.
Her feet go down to death;
her steps take hold on hell."
(Proverbs 5:3-5)

Chapter 31
The Strange Woman
Proverbs 2:16 -19; 5:3 -23; 7:5 -27

*T*HE BOOK OF PROVERBS has several verses in several different chapters which speak about the strange woman. I have a talk which I often give to teenage girls entitled, "How Strange Are You?" My daughter, Jaclynn, saw me studying this talk and was intrigued by the title. She teasingly said, "Mom, you are real strange." Jaclynn interpreted the word strange to mean weird or peculiar. The strange woman in the book of Proverbs is not peculiar; she is an impure or an immoral woman.

Though I have lived in my 34 years a pure and upstanding moral life, I was convicted as I saw some similarities between myself and the strange woman. It was a help for me to study her and, after studying her, I made a few changes in my own life. If I needed to learn from her, I have a strong feeling that each of my readers needs to learn from her also. Because of this, I would like to describe her to you.

The first thing I wish to do in this chapter is to cause you to desire **not** to be like her. Proverbs 5 tells us the end of the man who goes to the strange woman. I would think that the strange woman's end would be very similar. Because of this, allow me to share these passages with you.

1. **The strange woman experiences a loss of honor and respect**. *"Lest thou give thine honor unto others."* (Proverbs

5:9a) In other words, she loses her testimony and her good reputation. This is the first thing that happens to any girl who begins to live immorally.

In March of 1992 I published my first book entitled, *A Wife's Purpose*. My first sale of the book was at the nationwide Pastors' School at my own church, First Baptist Church of Hammond, Indiana. My good friend, Pam Wallace, was available to sell my books, but I spent some time at the book table signing autographs. One afternoon while standing at the table, we overheard a man talking to another lady about buying my book. His words went something like this: "If you knew Cindy Schaap's testimony, you would buy that book."

In all of our lives, there are words which we hear over and over again which have little personal meaning in our lives until something is said or something happens to give them personal meaning. When I heard that man discussing my book that day, the word *testimony* took on a new and very personal meaning in my own life. How thankful I am that to this point in my life, the Lord has preserved my testimony. I treasure the richness of a good testimony. How sad to have lived in such a way as to have a poor testimony with others.

2. **The strange woman chooses friends who do not really love her**. *"And thy years unto the cruel."* (Proverbs 5:9b) Just as the man who succumbs to the strange woman is being used by her, so the strange woman chooses this same type of friends. They will use her and then cruelly leave her. I read in a magazine several years ago about an actress who said that she did not watch television and she did not allow her children to watch television. She would not allow them to watch her own television program. Why? Because it was filled with things which were not good for them to see. Yet she makes her money and her living by acting on television. This is the way of the stars of television as well as the rock music stars. They are not truly the friends of those whom they entertain. They do what they know is not best for their followers if that is necessary to make a lot of money. They do not love their followers; they simply are using

their followers.

3. **The strange woman pays a high price for her sin**. *"Lest strangers be filled with thy wealth."* (Proverbs 5:10a) The man who goes to a strange woman for pleasure gives his money to her. However, the sins in which the strange woman takes part can also be costly. Sin is expensive! The wicked woman gives more and more money to the drugs, cigarettes, alcohol or music to which she is addicted. She increases her need for her sin and spends more and more money, until she is left to live in poverty. Who gets her money? Those entertainers and salesman, those "friends" who have used her.

4. **The strange woman's rewards will go to others**. *"And thy labors be in the house of a stranger."* (Proverbs 5:10b) The rewards which should have been hers will go to others.

5. **The strange woman will mourn with regret that she did not do what was right**. *"And thou mourn at the last, when thy flesh and thy body are consumed."* (Proverbs 5:11) She will especially mourn as she sees sin take away her health. We have diseases such as AIDS, emphysema, lung cancer, etc. to remind of the effect of sin and immorality on our health.

6. **The strange woman loses, at the last, her chance for recovery**. *"I was almost in all evil in the midst of the congregation and assembly."* (Proverbs 5:14) God is always willing to forgive and to rebuild a life, but once a lady has gone further and further into sin, it becomes very difficult and almost impossible to overcome the bondage of sin. It is much easier to say "no" to sin in the first place.

7. **The strange woman loses her life**. *"Her house is the way to hell, going down to the chambers of death."* (Proverbs 7:27) The last thing the strange woman loses is her life and if she is not saved, she must suffer eternally in hell. Few are the women who live long lives when they have been impure in their living.

I don't believe that I have just described a future that any of my readers would desire. I know it is the opposite of what I desire for my future. Because of this, let us consider the traits and behavior which would bring a woman to this horrifying end.

- **The strange woman says things she doesn't mean, especially as a means of getting her own way**. *"To deliver thee from the strange woman, even from the stranger which flattereth with her words."* (Proverbs 2:16) The Bible says she flattereth with her lips. You may say that you have never said anything to a member of the opposite sex in order to get your way sexually with him. But have you ever told a man "I love you" only to discover later you did not mean it? I advise Christian teenage girls to save these words for one man. Have you wives ever said something to your husband which was untrue or pure flattery in order to be allowed to spend some money? We must be careful that we say what we mean and that we mean what we say. We must not exaggerate or, worse than that, tell a deliberate untruth.

- **The strange woman doesn't respect God's covenants**. *"Which forsaketh the guide of her youth, and forgetteth the covenant of her God."* (Proverbs 2:17) She has no respect for the commandments of or the vows made unto God. She does not respect things such as the marriage vows. Each Christian girl must take very seriously the covenant of marriage between a man and a woman. She must be very cautious about the way she behaves around a married man or around **any** man if she is a married woman.

- **The strange woman does not accept reprimands**. *"She is loud and stubborn; her feet abide not in her house."* (Proverbs 7:11) This is one of her characteristics which caused me to say "Ouch" a little bit. Though my husband is very gentle and patient with me, occasionally he has to reprimand me about something. I am sometimes hesitant to accept his rebuke or advice and tend to be defensive. Since studying the strange woman, I have tried to respond more often with a soft answer and with a meek and quiet spirit. I do not wish to go even a little ways down the strange woman's road.

I wonder how well most teenage girls accept the rebukes of

their parents to clean their rooms better, to be more respectful. If they rebel and take every suggestion sensitively, they have started down a wrong road, the strange woman's road.

• **The strange woman changes to fit in with those around her**. *"Lest thou shouldest ponder the path of life, her ways are moveable, that thou canst not know them."* (Proverbs 5:6) You never know what kind of mood she will be in. She may be kind; she may be unkind. She may act very spiritual **if** she is around spiritual people. She changes to unspiritual when she gets around the wrong crowd. I knew at least one girl like this in high school. Her adult life has not been very pleasant.

• **The strange woman is uncomfortable when people talk about spiritual things**. (Proverbs 5:6) One of the reasons she changes so much is to keep people from pondering the spiritual things which would hinder her from doing evil with them. She does not like those around her to think about spiritual things. I wonder how comfortable most average Christian teenage girls are talking about spiritual things with others. If they are uncomfortable, they should try comparing themselves with God's Word and see how they measure up. They may be a lot like the strange woman.

• **The strange woman doesn't honor her parents**. *"For the goodman is not at home, he is gone a long journey."* (Proverbs 7:19) The verse in Proverbs chapter 2 tells us that she *"forsaketh the guide of her youth."* The word *forsake* does not imply disobedience, but rather neglect. This means that a girl can be obedient to her parents and still be like a strange woman if she is neglecting to honor them. In Proverbs chapter 7, the strange woman takes advantage of her father's absence in order to do things behind his back of which she knows he would not approve. She is disloyal to her parents.

• **The strange woman is loud**. *"She is loud and stubborn; her feet abide not in her house."* (Proverbs 7:11) I teach my students at Hyles-Anderson College that it is fine for a girl to be loud in a crowd at a basketball game. It is wonderful for her to enthusiastically cheer for that which is right or as a way to honor a great Christian leader. However, a Christian girl should not be loud personally, especially when there are men around. This is froward behavior and will lead to immoral actions.

• **The strange woman is unscheduled, and she distracts busy people**. *"For she sitteth at the door of her house, on a seat in the high places of the city, To call passengers who go right on their ways."* (Proverbs 9:14, 15) The best way to stay pure is to live by schedule. The best of Christians would get into trouble if their lives were full of idle time. This is human nature. Without the Holy Spirit's help and without a schedule, we would all be strange and immoral in our behavior.

I teach my students not to be social butterflies and not to yell out to people when they see them coming down the hallways at school, especially men. A lady can smile widely and be friendly without being inappropriately loud.

The people who will most often want to counsel over and over again with people, simply telling them problem after problem, are of the same type as the strange woman. They will waste the time of others. While I believe in seeking counsel in preparation for life's duties or for major decisions, I do not believe in spending much time going from person to person just talking with others about problems and wasting their time.

• **The strange woman is out late at night**. *"In the twilight, in the evening, in the black and dark night."* (Proverbs 7:9) All of us are tempted to do wrong when we are overtired. It is wise for every woman, no matter what her age, to have a curfew and a decent bedtime. This will prevent quarrels as well as immorality. Every lady who must leave a place late at night should go straight home.

• **The strange woman dresses immodestly**. *"And, behold, there met him a woman with the attire of an harlot, and subtil of heart."* (Proverbs 7:10) This verse tells us that the strange woman clothes herself with the *"attire of an harlot."* Since the Bible tells us that there is a certain type of clothing which is the clothing of a harlot, a woman should develop standards about dress from God's Word; and she should live by them consistently. This is good protection for her purity.

My dress standards are as follows: I believe a woman should not wear a swimsuit in front of anyone except her husband. (This **must** be the attire of a harlot. There is nothing left beyond it except nudity.) She should not wear pants or other mannish apparel. (If my husband could wear it except for size, I don't buy it! Clothing can be tailored, but it must have **something** which is distinctly feminine.) She should wear only dresses and skirts which cover her thighs and her bustline. Not only does clothing need to cover these things, but it should not draw undue attention to them through slits in skirts, tightness around hips or bust, etc.

- **The strange woman is forward**. *"So she caught him, and kissed him, and with an impudent face . . ."* (Proverbs 7:13) Some standards which I have and teach to prevent forwardness are as follows:

A.   Don't call boys on the telephone.
B.   Don't talk crassly about a boy's physical appearance.
C.   Don't touch boys.
D.   Don't follow a boy whom you are interested in dating. You may say "hello" to him or become acquainted with him by becoming involved with things in which he is involved, but I would not chase him.
E.   Don't lead in a dating relationship. I never sought out my husband until we were going steady and there was an understanding between us. If we talked, he walked up to me. I never walked up to him. I never assumed or stated feelings in our relationship until my husband had already stated his feelings.

- **The strange woman doesn't like to be at home**. *"Now is she without, now in the streets, and lieth in wait at every corner."* (Proverbs 7:12) An unmarried girl can avoid temptation by enjoying her home and her parents. She can find in them the security that she might be tempted to seek in an illicit sexual affair. Later, that security can be transferred to the husband God has for her.

• **The strange woman is unchaperoned**. *"For the goodman is not at home, he is gone a long journey."* (Proverbs 7:19) When two people love each other very much, it is natural for them to desire each other sexually. It is not God's plan for them to enjoy sex until after marriage. Sex before marriage hinders the enjoyment of sex after marriage. A girl can protect the enjoyment of her marriage romance by having a chaperone or by staying in places where there are a lot of people.

• **The strange woman uses improper body language**. *"A naughty person, a wicked man, walketh with a froward mouth. He winketh with his eyes, he speaketh with his feet, he teacheth with his fingers; Frowardness is in his heart, he deviseth mischief continually; he soweth discord."* (Proverbs 6:12-14) I once knew a former homosexual whom my husband won to the Lord. He told my husband that he can spot a homosexual in less than 5 seconds. I can sometimes detect a person's character in that same amount of time. How? By observing their body language. My book *A Wife's Purpose* has a chapter on faithfulness which deals with proper body language. A pure lady will be careful about her posture, her eye contact, her facial expressions, her walk, her tone of voice and her words when she is around the opposite sex.

The Bible says in Proverbs 22:3, *"A prudent man foreseeth the evil, and hideth himself: but the simple pass on, and are punished."* The dictionary definition of the word *prudent* is *careful to avoid errors, cautious, of sound judgment.*

If a Christian girl will avoid the errors discussed in this chapter, she will avoid the error of immorality in her life. She will avoid the sad and deadly end of the strange woman. She will live purely with no regrets. She will have the potential to live happily ever after in love with the one man God has for her.

The Proverbs 31 Lady —
A Lesson on Priorities

❧

"Who can find a virtuous woman?
for her price is far above rubies.
The heart of her husband doth safely trust in her,
so that he shall have no need of spoil.
She will do him good and not evil
all the days of her life."
(Proverbs 31:10-12)

Chapter 32
Proverbs 31 Lady
Proverbs 31:10 -31

*I*N THE LAST CHAPTER of Proverbs, we have a beautiful description of a virtuous woman. I have heard it used over and over again through my lifetime as an example to Christian wives. In this chapter, we find the priorities which every Christian wife should have in order to be a virtuous woman.

A WIFE'S MAIN PRIORITY SHOULD BE HER HUSBAND.

The Proverbs 31 lady has her husband as her first priority. She begins to be described in verse 10 as being of great value. Then right away in verse 11 and 12, her care for her husband is described. Verse 11 tells us that her husband trusts her. He trusts her with his feelings; he knows that she will not be moody, but that she will consistently treat him well. He trusts her with his reputation; he knows she will not criticize him or reveal his weaknesses. He trusts her with his money and his possessions. He knows that she will care properly for his children and for his personal possessions and that she will not squander his money. Proverbs 31 gives us a pretty good idea that a woman's first priority should be her husband. It also seems to tell us that all of the other priorities in our lives should be lived out in order to benefit our husbands.

The following are the priorities which a virtuous woman has in order to please her husband:

1. **Sewing and mending**. *"She seeketh wool, and flax, and worketh willingly with her hands."* (v. 13) *"She layeth her hands to the spindle, and her hands hold the distaff."* (v. 19)

2. **Grocery shopping**. *"She is like the merchants' ships; she bringeth her food from afar."* (v. 14)

3. **Food preparation**. *"She riseth also while it is yet night, and giveth meat to her household, and a portion to her maidens."* (v. 15)

4. **Gardening**. *"She considereth a field, and buyeth it: with the fruit of her hands she planteth a vineyard."* (v. 16)

5. **Exercise**. *"She girdeth her loins with strength, and strengtheneth her arms."* (v. 17) This verse talks about strength and may also refer to the strength she finds in her daily devotional life.

6. **Supplementing the family income**. *"She perceiveth that her merchandise is good: her candle goeth not out by night."* (v. 18) *"She maketh fine linen, and selleth it; and delivereth girdles unto the merchant."* (v. 24)

7. **Giving**. *"She stretcheth out her hand to the poor; yea, she reacheth forth her hands to the needy."* (v. 20)

8. **Caring for her family's health and appearance**. *"She is not afraid of the snow for her household: for all her household are clothed with scarlet."* (v. 21)

9. **Her own appearance**. *"She maketh herself coverings of tapestry; her clothing is silk and purple."* (v. 22)

10. **Watching over her children and those in her household**. *"She looketh well to the ways of her household, and eateth not the bread of idleness."* (v. 27)

11. **Reading and obtaining wisdom**. *"She openeth her mouth with wisdom; and in her tongue is the law of kindness."* (v. 26)

How fortunate the Christian wife is to have her household responsibilities outlined for her in the book of Proverbs.

One of my favorite verses in Proverbs 31 is verse 26. It tells us that the virtuous woman sets rules for herself regarding her tongue. Again, I believe she did this mainly as a way of pleasing her husband. What is the rule? It is the "law of kindness." We might rephrase this rule by repeating an old adage which says: "If you can't think of anything good to say, say **nothing** at all." We could also rephrase this law by stating two rules for marriage which I share in my book, *A Wife's Purpose*:

- Never say anything negative about your husband.

- Take every opportunity to say something positive about your husband.

Those two rules could include any of our loved ones. This is the kind of law by which the virtuous woman lived.

What is the end result of the woman who keeps her husband as her first priority?

1. **Her husband will have a good reputation**. *"Her husband is known in the gates, when he sitteth among the elders of the land."* (v. 23) Why? His wife cares for his home and children properly which gives him the freedom to care for other things. His very appearance is one of cleanliness and sharpness because of his wife's good care of him. Also, he is well-loved and respected by others because his wife has been guarding his reputation by living by the law of kindness.

2. **The virtuous woman is also honored by others**. *"Strength and honour are her clothing; and she shall rejoice in time to come."* (v. 25) This is not her motive. Her goal is to work hard, and her motive is to please her husband; but a woman who works hard and who is kind to others, a woman who develops herself in all the areas mentioned, will be honored by others.

3. **The virtuous woman becomes strong**. *"Strength and honour are her clothing; and she shall rejoice in time to come."* (v. 25) The hard work of homemaking and the scheduling of the many necessary tasks make a woman stronger mentally as well as physically. Her diligence in striving to become the kind of wife who would please her husband also causes her to develop some strength emotionally and spiritually.

4. **The virtuous woman is loved and praised by her family**. *"Her children arise up, and call her blessed; her husband also, and he praiseth her."* (v. 28) She receives what every woman desires most — not the applause of crowds, but the genuine love and appreciation of her family. Her children say, "My mom is the greatest mom in the whole world." Her husband says, "I'm proud of my wife, and I love her!" Does she get this love and appreciation by asking for it? No, she receives it by being a servant and by working hard.

5. **The works of the virtuous woman speak for themselves**. *"Give her of the fruit of her hands; and let her own works praise her in the gates."* (v. 31) She accomplishes so much through her hard work and through what she has done for other people that she does not need to boast. The fruit of her own labors gives her the self satisfaction she needs. She has a good reputation and bears a positive testimony because of the fruit of her labors.

6. **The virtuous woman develops an inward excellence which surpasses outward beauty or popularity**. *"Favour is deceitful, and beauty is vain: but a woman that feareth the LORD, she shall be praised."* (v. 30) Outward beauty does not last or satisfy, and people can sometimes become popular for some very wrong reasons. A wife who fears, respects and reverences the Lord will be praised.

In 1994, it has become distasteful to many woman to fulfill the duties of homemaking. We even have a rise in the number of men who live as house husbands. Many are the women who have full-time careers and who insist on their husbands doing 50 percent of the household chores and child care. Yet the Bible clearly teaches that the main keeper at home should be the wife. Her husband may help her as a voluntary display of his love for her, but the virtuous woman should find pleasure in making her home a lovely place for her husband. Even in the 1990's, I have heard men say that home is their favorite place to be. I have no doubt that these men have wives who are diligent in their homemaking.

Lastly, Proverbs 31 tells us that the virtuous woman fears the Lord. Should the Lord then be her first priority? The mention of her fear of the Lord is at the very end of the chapter, almost as an afterthought. Why? I have learned in my own experience that the more priority I give to my husband, the more I love and desire to obey God. In fact, the more I love my husband, the more I love God. God placed the husband as the main authority in a wife's life; therefore, he is, in some ways, like God to her. Because of this, the husband should always be the center of his wife's life.

If the other responsibilities of her life are performed in order to please her husband — whether that includes a part-time job, housekeeping, child rearing, or enhancing her own outward appearance — those responsibilities will all stay in their proper priority. She will not become obsessed or overly concerned with any one responsibility when all are fulfilled with the purpose of pleasing her first priority, her husband.

Also, as the wife seeks to please her husband, she will discover — as I have — that she cannot please him through any of her labors unless she seeks out the wisdom of God through consistent time with God in prayer and in the Bible. In her desire to please her husband, she will become a greater Christian without becoming pious or self-righteous to her husband.

What a challenge to be a virtuous woman! It is a great challenge to keep the husband always as the first priority in our lives. It is after we have given him proper priority that our love and pleasure in being his wife is fully developed. It is a challenge to do the work which is needed to be a helpmeet for a husband. Yet when we see its end, we realize it is truly worth the challenge — not only as a means of expressing our love to our husbands, but especially as a means of expressing our love for Christ.

Gomer —
A Lesson on Commitment

❦

"But he, being full of compassion,
forgave their iniquity, and destroyed them not:
yea, many a time turned he his anger away,
and did not stir up all his wrath.
For he remembered that they were but flesh;
a wind that passeth away,
and cometh not again."
(Psalm 78:38, 39)

Chapter 33
Gomer
Hosea 1, 2, 3

A Tribute to Jack

HOSEA WAS A PROPHET of God who prophesied from the time he was a very young man until he was an old man. God commanded Hosea to take a wife of whoredoms. Hosea married Gomer, and she bore three children. The first child was a son named Jezreel. *Jezreel* means *scattered of God*. This meaning signified what was about to happen to Israel as a result of their wandering from God. It also signified what was going to happen to Gomer.

Hosea and Gomer's second child was a girl whom they named *Lo-ruhamah* which means *not beloved*. This name reflects Gomer's attitude toward her children and God's attitude toward wandering Israel. The third child (a girl) was named *Lo-ammi* which means *not my people*.

During Hosea and Gomer's marriage, Gomer displayed a lack of compassion by leaving her husband and children to commit whoredom with other men. Hosea was committed to Gomer, and he tried everything to get her to return and to become faithful to him. Hosea pleaded with his wife to return. He asked his three children to plead with her. Because Gomer's children were "not beloved" by her, she continued in her sin and in her wanderings.

The goal of Gomer's wanderings was to obtain money and material things. While she went looking for those things, ironically, it was Hosea who secretly provided for her needs. This is so like most people in the world. They neglect the things of God and His will in order to become materially wealthy while failing to realize that all good things come from God.

Hosea desired to take these material things away from Gomer in order to hasten her return to him, but Gomer did not return. Finally, probably after many long years of sin and a hard life, Hosea bought Gomer for fifteen pieces of silver when she was being auctioned as a slave. By this time, I'm sure that Gomer did not have much to offer Hosea. I doubt that she was physically very lovely or strong. Her mind and emotions as well as her spirit had probably been ravaged by years of sin. I'm sure there was no money set aside which she could share with Hosea. Her quest for material things surely ended in the poverty of sin.

But Hosea had entered into a covenant of marriage with Gomer, and he was committed to that covenant. I have learned a lot about commitment through my life, especially through my 15 years of marriage.

When I began dating my husband, Jack Schaap, 17 years ago, it only took a couple of dates for me to understand that my new friend was very committed to me. In fact, after our second date, my dear friend, Robyn Foster Steiner, said something like this to me, "Cindy, that man loves you. He always has, and he always will." I was seventeen at the time, Robyn was eighteen, and Jack was nineteen. Those were strange words for Robyn to speak to me, I'm sure. Yet they describe exactly the way I felt when the relationship between Jack and me had only begun. I felt a love that came from God and could have been better labeled as commitment. I have never known a more committed or a more stable man than Jack Schaap.

I was not as committed as Jack was when we began our courtship. I had dated several young men by the time I met him. I was the daughter of a famous preacher, and I did not fit the bill very well. This left me insecure and in need of much learning on the subject of committed love.

I have two wonderful parents who both were there for me during my childhood. Both are great Christians, and they loved me closely and gave me their best as parents. Yet, God had much to teach me about love; and He has used through the years His finest tool for teaching me, and that is the wonderful institution of marriage. Through my marriage and my wonderful husband, I have hopefully learned to be as committed to Jack as he is to me.

I remember a particular instance in our dating life when Jack taught me a fundamental lesson on his commitment and on God's. Jack and I dated for nine months before we ever had an argument. I put my best foot forward at all times during those first nine months, and everything went wonderfully.

It wasn't long, however, until the real Cindy Hyles began to show; and Jack and I had our first argument. My insecurity began to show and so, in a small way, did some temper. I was afraid that I would lose Jack when he saw my humanness, and I was thoroughly disgusted with myself for behaving wrongly. Jack quickly forgave me, but I found it hard to forgive myself.

After several moments of berating myself, Jack did something that none of the young men I dated before him had ever done. He opened the Bible and ministered unto my need. I have never been able to read the passage he showed me without cherishing the memory of that evening. So many times since then Jack has ministered to my needs, and there are so many verses I now come across in my personal Bible reading which remind me of his committed love.

The passage which he showed me sums up the description of the love Hosea had for Gomer, the love Jack has for Cindy and, most of all, it summarizes the amazing love which God has for all of us.

It was Psalms 78:38 and 39, which says, *"But he, being full of compassion, forgave their iniquity, and destroyed them not:*

yea, many a time turned he his anger away, and did not stir up all his wrath. For he remembered that they were but flesh; a wind that passeth away, and cometh not again."

These verses remind me of the kind of commitment and compassion that can cause a man like Hosea to forgive a wife of whoredom time and time again. It describes the kind of love and commitment I have experienced in my own marriage, and I believe it describes the kind of commitment God meant for each married partner to have for the other.

It is easy to bask in the glory of having someone who has such commitment for us. It is much harder to enjoy giving that type of commitment to another person. Sometimes, the forgiven one can become proud and vain once her sins are in the past; and she can begin to expect perfection from the very spouse who so graciously forgave her own faults. How tragic! I owe a lifetime of commitment to Jack Schaap after what he has done to overlook my weaknesses. I would be wrong to be unwilling to overlook some weakness on his part.

But the story of Hosea and Gomer does not just depict the type of commitment each marriage partner should have for the other; it also depicts the kind of commitment which God has for His children.

We, like Gomer, are prone to wander from our Lord. So often, it is the desire for material gain and for things of this world which cause us to stray. We fail to realize that it is our relationship with God which provides all that is good and that, if we leave Him full, we may very well come back empty. Yet God does not leave us empty because He has lost His compassion and commitment for us. Rather, He leaves us empty so that we might return to our love relationship with Him. He misses us when we have gone.

As stated earlier in this chapter, the very names of Hosea and Gomer's children were a symbol of God's disgust with His children when they backslide. Further on in the book of Hosea, though, God changed the names of the daughters. Lo-ruhamah (not beloved) became *Ruhamah* which means *beloved* and Lo-ammi (not my people) became *Ammi* which means *my people*. God cannot stay angry with His children long, though they be the children of whoredoms. His compassion to them and His commitment to them is too great! God intended our marriages to picture such love. Why cannot we, as forgiven sinners, love in our marriages as God has loved us?

I am grateful to God for His commitment to me! I am grateful to my husband, Jack Schaap, for giving me that same godly type of commitment. In doing so, Jack has taught me lessons of infinite and eternal value. He has taught me about God.

I love you, Jack. Thank you for teaching me the greatest lesson for wives that can be learned from the Bible.

Other books available from Sheep Publications:

A Wife's Purpose
by Cindy Schaap

Common Sense Christian Dating
by Dr. Jack Schaap